Ed & JJ
Happy Reading
Thanks for your Support.

THE CAULKERS OF SIERRA LEONE

The Story of a Ruling Family and Their Times

Imodale Caulker-Burnett

A Caulker Descendant

Copyright © 2010 by Imodale Caulker-Burnett.

Library of Congress Control Number: 2010915862
ISBN: Hardcover   978-1-4568-0241-7
       Softcover   978-1-4568-0240-0
       Ebook   978-1-4568-0242-4

All rights reserved. No part of this book may be reproduced or transmitted in any form or by any means, electronic or mechanical, including photocopying, recording, or by any information storage and retrieval system, without permission in writing from the copyright owner.

This book was printed in the United States of America.

To order additional copies of this book, contact:
Xlibris Corporation
1-888-795-4274
www.Xlibris.com
Orders@Xlibris.com
88986

Contents

Forward 8
Acknowledgments 12
Introduction 14

Part I
The History

Chapter I—Early History of Sierra Leone and the Origins
    of the Caulker Family 22
Chapter II—The European Ancestors 34

Part II
The Caulkers of Sierra Leone

Chapter III—Thomas Corker and Senora Doll 40
Chapter IV—Legends and Stories of the Old Kagbor Chiefdom 47
Chapter V—The Cleveland Connection 56
Chapter VI—The Influence of Education and Religion 62

Part III
Challenges in the family

Chapter VII—The Corkers/Caulkers and the Slave Trade 84
Chapter VIII—The Caulker Wars 96

Part IV
The Ancestors and their Influence

Chapter IX—The Ancestors and their influence 124
Chapter X—The Last Word 132

Appendices

Appendix I—Summary of the Caulker Rulers—from 1780-1999 139
Appendix II—A Walking Tour Around the Old Town of Shenge 158
Appendix III—The Treaties 163
Appendix VI—The Caulker Manuscripts 171

Resources 206
Picture Gallery 209
Author's Bio 228

DEDICATION

This book is dedicated to the Memory of
My Beloved Father,
Dr. Richard Edmund Kelfa-Caulker of Mambo House
*First African Principal of the Albert Academy,
First Ambassador to the United States and
the United Nations after Independence
High Commissioner to the Court of St. James
Principal, Schlenker Secondary School, Port Loko,
Ambassador to Liberia*

He loved to share stories of the Caulkers with his children and always spoke proudly of his village Mambo, no matter where he was or who his audience happened to be.

He struggled to find a balance between being African and living in the Western world which, for his time, was a difficult challenge. Yet he emerged as a distinguished African, who served his country with pride and dignity, and succeeded in making us, his children, proud of who we are—CAULKERS—PROUD AFRICANS.

Forward

Sierra Leone has waited long for histories written by men and women of the soil. Their emergence has been slow, with only one or two published family stories. A history of the Caulkers comes therefore, as a timely, valuable and rewarding contribution to supplying this long-felt need. Its apparently modest dimensions and the goal of informing young family members are deceptive in the sense that the depth and implications for the author's countrymen are far-reaching. Imodale Caulker-Burnett sets out to tell the story of the Caulker dynasty from its C17th Afro-European beginnings to the present day, through the vicissitudes of wars and family feuds, marriage customs and traditions. She transforms what seems like a mammouth task into a text that reads easily and pleasantly. There is a careful balance between historical detail and interesting or amusing anecdotes, so that it is far from being a dry historical treatise.

Encompassing all the manifold and diverse accounts of action and reaction are her strong sense of pride and love for her family and her deep devotion to it. The reader is never allowed to lose sight of this but the narrative never becomes over-emotional or trite. Even the picture gallery at the end focuses on achievement rather than sentiment.

The historical content is supported by additional source material such as 'The Caulker Manuscripts' in the Appendiix. This should stimulate the scholarly reader in search of further authentic data. It is worth noting that these manuscripts are reproduced here for public consumption, most probably for the first time, which gives the work an aura of novelty.

In trying to satisfy her own curiosity about her family's story, the author will surely awaken a kindred desire in other members of great families to delve into the past, thus enlightening the present age and posterity on the role of their ancestos in the development of their country. Her meeting with distant 'cousins' in the USA triggered her passion for more knowledge and the sharing of that knowledge.

This book will surely find a place in home, school, college and university as a reliable source of information, not only about the Caulker family. It also deals with significant issues and events of different periods including the Slave Trade and the Hut Tax War as experienced by individuals and communities in the Sherbro chiefdoms. The times they lived through were common to all Sierra Leoneans and marked the different stages of our country's journey to nationhood over a period of four centuries.

Rachel Lulu Wright, Daughter of Rachel Coker(nee Caulker)
Former Head, Department of Modern Languages
Fourah Bay College
University of Sierra Leone

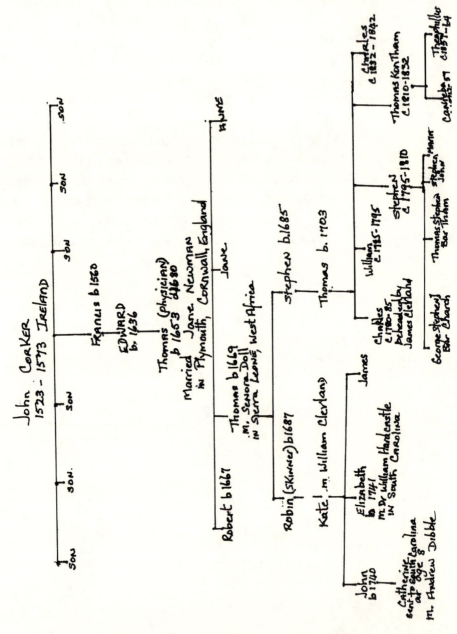

The Corkers of Ireland/Caulkers of Sierra Leone
The connection

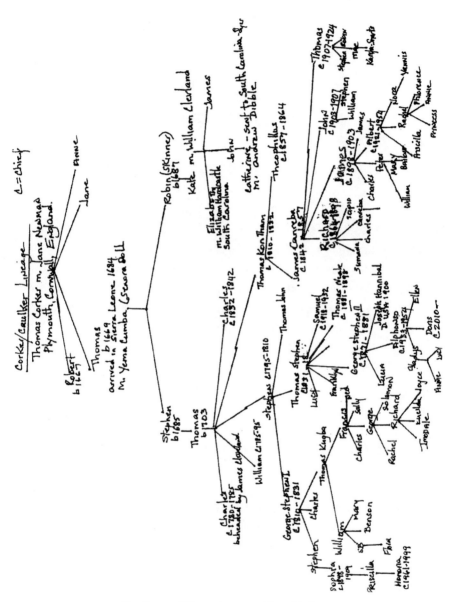

Caulkers of Sierra Leone—The chiefs

Acknowledgments

I especially wish to thank my Uncle Bart (referred to by his full name, Stephen Bar Thebin Caulker, in this book), who has always been willing to share the information he collected, when he defended his claim of the right to carry the Corker family coat-of-arms, as a descendant of Thomas Corker Jr. of Falmouth, United Kingdom. In 1981 he was awarded a certificate of confirmation of the Corker coat-of-arms, from the College of Arms in Dublin Castle, Ireland.

A big thank you to Uncle Francis, for sharing his invaluable work on the Caulker Family. The passages from his unpublished historical novel about the Caulkers, have added character and humor to this story.

Thank you to the late Christopher Fyfe, T.N. Goddard and A. Peter Kup, who took the time to record much of the early Corker/Caulker history in their works on Sierra Leone. They demonstrated the contribution of the Caulkers to the development of Sierra Leone, and provided a starting point from which to capture our past.

Thanks to those who provided verbal history and/or resource material. Especially the Myers sisters—Elsie Mae Kallon, and Laurel Turay, Dr. Hedrick Barlay, Dr. Patrick Caulker, historian Dr. Joseph Allie, Mr. Frank Karefa-Smart, and Paramount Chief Charles Caulker of Bompeh chiefdom. Thanks also to all those who have contributed precious photographs of their loved ones, thus adding value and credibility to the book

Special thanks to my husband Clive who has supported this work and has patiently listened to the many stories about the Caulkers. He has also been willing to attend many Caulker Descendant events, in order to understand the family into which he has married.

Thank you to my nephew Mark Hunter (son of Yema Lucilda Hunter) who designed the book cover. His talent as a Graphic Artist is greatly appreciated.

Finally, thank you to all those who have patiently read and critiqued the various manuscripts which have been handed to them—my sister Yema Lucilda Hunter, who worked so hard on editing the book, my cousins Lulu Wright, the late Dr. Enid Forde, Elsie Mae Kallon and Laurel Turay, and Annie Bangura, Paramount Chief Rev. Doris Lenga-Caulker Gbabior II of Kagboro Chiefdom, Paramount Chief Charles Caulker of Bompeh chiefdom, Mr. Frank Karefa-Smart, Dr. Joe Allie professor of History at Fourah Bay College, and Dr. Hedrick Barlay. Their comments and suggestions have been invaluable.

IC-B

Introduction

In 1985, I received a telephone call from Atlanta Georgia, in the United States of America, inviting me to participate in the Nauddin-Dibble family reunion. Since I had never heard of the Nauddin-Dibbles, I was very surprised, especially when I was told by the caller, the late Dr. James Palmer that we were cousins. It turned out that the Naudin-Dibble family had traced its roots back to William Clevland and Kate Corker (one of our ancestors) of Sierra Leone, West Africa, and they were interested in making their African connection. At the time, I knew almost nothing about the Cleveland family, except what I had read in history books, so this was a great opportunity to learn about them

At the reunion I represented the Caulkers of Sierra Leone and my cousin Rosemarie Cleveland-Williams, (whom I had met for the first time here in the States), represented the Clevelands of Sierra Leone. We spent a lot of time reviewing both family histories, so that we could understand some of the issues which seemed to have created such a large chasm that had lasted so long. At the family dinner, according to African tradition, I poured a libation to honor all the ancestors and asked for help and support, as we tried to heal the breach between the two families. The experience was enlightening, and it was indeed a privilege for this African American family and my family to connect through our history. Since then, members of that family have attended a few of our reunions, and we have attended some of their reunions.

When I saw the Naudin-Dibble family tree which was drawn in the shape of a large tree on a huge piece of canvas, I knew I had to make one just like it for the Caulkers. From then on, each time I visited Sierra Leone or met a relative whom I did not know, I tried to get as much information as I could. My big chance came when the Caulker

Family in Sierra Leone had its first family reunion in Freetown on New Year's Day 1997 ordered by the then Paramount Chief Madam Honoria Bailor-Caulker of Kagboro Chiefdom. It was truly a day for reminiscing, a day of meeting new family members, and family elders. For a little while, the family could pretend we were in Shenge or Rotifunk—the family seats in the two chiefdoms, and remember the 'good old' days. It was a day of healing for those who were displaced and disconnected because of the rebel war which was raging up country. It was indeed an oasis—a pleasant break from the unpleasantness of war. It was also a good opportunity for me to collect information which I needed about the Caulker family.

Having made the African Connection with the Nauddin-Dibbles, it became clear to me, that promoting Unity within our own family, had to include learning about and clearing up of century old grudges before we could begin the process of healing the many differences which seem to exist between all the family groups—Caulker/Corkers and Clevelands, the Bompeh Caulkers and Shenge Caulkers, the Shenge Caulkers and the Mambo Caulkers and those within families. In the past these quarrels ended up in wars which, to this day, seem to have left an underlying tension between the family branches.

After Paramount Chief Madam Honoria Bailor-Caulker died in 1999, many of us who attended the funeral services in Washington D.C. came to the realization that the family was good at gathering for funerals, but we almost never gathered in such numbers for family celebrations. This needed to change. If the goal was to promote family unity, it was important to gather just for fun, and in the process, share our knowledge of the family history with the younger ones. We decided to start by having family reunions at which this information could be disseminated. We pledged at that time to plan our first family reunion. A Committee of three—myself, and two cousins, Hannah (Nelson) Olu-Nylander, and Lawrence Caulker, set about planning our first reunion.

On the weekend of Halloween, October 30th 1999, the first Caulker family reunion was held in the United States. Over one hundred Caulkers from the US, and Canada, attended, including family Elder, Stephen Bar Thebin Caulker (Uncle Bart) who came all the way from England. There were new cousins, uncles and aunts to meet, and I created a family tree at which those present could trace their lineage. Booklets with historical information, as well as Tee shirts, were given to all registrants.

The Caulker Family tree, created by Imodale Caulker-Burnett 1999

At the end of the weekend, there were various expressions of gratitude for what everyone said was a great experience. One family member, Stephen John Caulker, who had arrived from Canada, had neither heard the history of the Caulkers, nor had he ever been to Sierra Leone. In fact, he had no idea that he had such a large extended family. He wrote:

> "To begin with, all I knew was my immediate family. I only met my grandparents once before they died and that was many years ago. Other than some old photographs, it was all I knew. In one weekend my family has grown in leaps and bounds. My feelings of pride and self worth have been changed forever . . . That we have been found by such an extended family has been a blessing . . . It is nice to know that my immediate family is not alone in this world . . ." Stephen.

Another said:

> "I am glad to know more about Daddy Willie's family and to be a part of this wonderful family . . ." Katie

Another said:

> "Aunty, I am glad I came to this reunion because now I know who I am . . ." David

Yet another wrote,

> "I must thank you so much for this reunion. I went through the booklet and it has really helped me come to terms with myself, my character, my spirit, my mind and my soul. Thank you . . ." Sonia

These responses, indicate that we cannot underestimate the needs of our young people. They are eager for the information which many of us older ones, were given by the generations before.

Why this book?

One of my father's favorite sayings to me as I prepared to leave for college in the United States was, *"If you do not know where you are going, remember where you have come from."* As a young girl, I did not appreciate the significance of what he meant, but over the years, I have come to understand its meaning. Now I embrace it as a guide for my own life.

I believe that when young people learn about their family and its history, it gives them a perspective from which they can pattern their own lives, no matter where they are. It also provides everyone with an understanding and an appreciation of the choices we do have in this life. Choices based on who we are and where we come from. Many of our elders knew the importance of imparting family history. They recognized the fact that if their children went overseas for higher education, or for any other reason, there was a great chance that the history would be lost. So they frequently told stories about the family to their children and grand children. I remember, in the 1950's whenever my family went to visit our grandparents in the village of Mambo, it seemed that at every stop along the way, we were introduced to a seemingly unending line of members of the extended family, with an attempt at explaining how they were related. At Mambo, in the evenings, after the lanterns were lit and the mosquitoes sprayed, we enjoyed sitting on the veranda on moonlit nights listening to our grandfather and uncles tell stories about 'The old days'. In their stories, their pride and devotion to family came through loud and clear. This is how I learned about the family history.

Sierra Leone gained its independence in 1961, but unfortunately by the end of that decade things began to change. By the 1980's the slow exodus of Sierra Leoneans, which had begun several years before as more and more people had the opportunity to go abroad for higher education, increased. More and more educated Sierra Leoneans left the country for greener pastures. The villages became deserted. The elders had passed on, and their children rarely visited. Now, many of those who went overseas are raising new generations of Caulkers far away from home. Today there are at least two or more generations of Caulkers, who do not know their family history.

In an article written in 1999 for the 'Genealogy' newsletter of the Nauddin-Dibble family (the African-American descendants of Kate Corker/Caulker and William Clevland), Will Yoreau Goins, a descendant, presents reasons why it is important to learn about a family's history. He writes:

> "There is something empowering about knowing your history. When you know your own personal history, it makes you feel like you really have a place in this world. A sense of rootedness, a sense of belonging . . . To understand yourself, you have to know where you come from . . ."

In a similar vein, the late Mr. Max Bailor, a Caulker family elder, in a letter to the Caulker Descendants as they met for their first Family Reunion in the USA said,

> "The past is our Heritage,
> The present is our responsibility
> The Future is our challenge."

Except for the *"Caulker Manuscripts"* which were written by George Maximillan Domingo,—Chiefdom Speaker during the reign of Madam Sophia Neale-Caulker 1898-1908) and a couple of small unpublished books, *"A short story of the Kagbor Chiefdom"*, by Mr. Lionel Tower, and *"The Caulkers "*—an unpublished historical novel by Mr. Francis Caulker, little has been written about the Caulkers of Sierra Leone by any member of the 'African' family. Those who knew the family history, such as the late Mr. John Caulker, who until his death in 2006 was considered a 'walking Caulker historian', seemed to want to guard their knowledge, instead of giving it up for documentation. Fortunately, because of the strong European presence in the family's history a good deal of information about the Caulkers, can be found in History books on Sierra Leone, written by European historians such as Christopher Fyfe, Peter Kup, T.N.Goddard, E. Louise of the Nauddin-Dibble family and some of the missionaries of the United Brethren in Christ (UBC) Church. With their accounts and the information gleaned from stories told by our parents, grandparents and other relatives, I have been able to trace our roots back to the 1500's. I believe this is a gift which should not be taken for granted. The challenge I now have, is to pass this information on. Unless such knowledge is shared, as family elders pass on, future generations will be left with even fewer resources, to learn about their heritage.

The Rebel War, which raged in Sierra Leone between 1991 and 2001, has increased the danger of this happening, as many people all over the country including members of the Caulker family lost valuable heirlooms, artifacts, historical documents and photographs.

As we begin this journey of discovery, I think there are three aspects of our history we should examine.

* First, we should understand and have an image of what Sierra Leone was like, before the Europeans arrived and the Portuguese named it in 1462.
* Next, we should know what the English and the African sides were like. Where each side came from, how the two sides met, what life was like for them, how they dealt with it, and how they handled their responsibilities as leaders.

* Finally, as descendants, we should be asking the questions, where do we go from here? How do we use the heritage we have been given?

I hope the information I have given in this book, will help to answer some of these questions, As Paramount Chief Charles Caulker of Bompeh Chiefdom points out,

> *We must not forget that we are all descended from a European merchant and an African Queen. We have all been born into royalty, whether we like it or not. Regardless of the fact that, one is from Bompeh or Kagboro, we are first ONE FAMILY. By virtue of our heritage as Caulkers, we will always have a role to play in the development of our country Sierra Leone. It is a role which demands Family Unity.*

The Caulker family is a very large one, whose members are scattered all over the world. As a result, there are Caulker children who know little or nothing of their family's history. This book is mainly for them. This project is only the beginning of the search for who we really are, and I hope it will be used as a tool for restoring and reclaiming the gift our ancestors have left us.—A proud Heritage.

IC-B

Part I

The History

Chapter I

Early History of Sierra Leone and the Origins of the Caulker Family

For thousands of years, Africa has been a source of interest to Europeans. Well before the Portuguese arrived, there were stories of one **Hanno**, a Carthaginian, who supposedly arrived on the western coast in 500 BC. He may have been the first known explorer to ever arrive on the West African Coast, at an area now known as the "Bay of Sierra Leone". As the story goes, Hanno traveled under the command of the senate of Carthage (today's Tunisia), with 60 ships, and 30,000 men and women in search of new trading outlets. (*Goddard 1925*)

Although no one really knew about Hanno's journey, adventurers who had read the written reports of his voyages accepted the stories as truth. It is now believed that the story of Hanno's voyage down the West African Coast may have been a myth for many reasons. For instance, the weather they described on their arrival, was more common further north near Morocco. The same was true of the descriptions of some of the things they saw. (*Kup1961*)

Around the 1400's the Portuguese arrived claiming they were coming to "Spread Christianity". In reality, they had heard that gold lay in large quantities in the middle of Africa and they were determined to get it before anyone else did. Many of them wrote about their experiences and made maps of what they had seen, but they kept their maps and the knowledge they had gained a secret, so that rival countries would not begin to compete for the wealth they had discovered. And so, over many centuries, as they went about in their search for a route to India and for the gold they had heard of, the west coast of Africa remained mysterious to those explorers who came across this intriguing land. *(Kup 1961)*

Some reports suggest that Portuguese explorers had sighted what is now the Sierra Leone Coast in 1446. But it was not until 1462 when another Portuguese sailor, Pedro da Cintra arrived at this same coast on his way to India, that it was named Serra Lyoa, because of its impressive mountain range which they thought resembled a pride of lions. Da Cintra's ship, arrived at night in the middle of a storm and the thunder and lightning caused he and his crew to think they were seeing this pride of lions and hearing their roars, hence the name "Serra Lyoa"—The Lion Mountain" *(Fyfe 1964)*

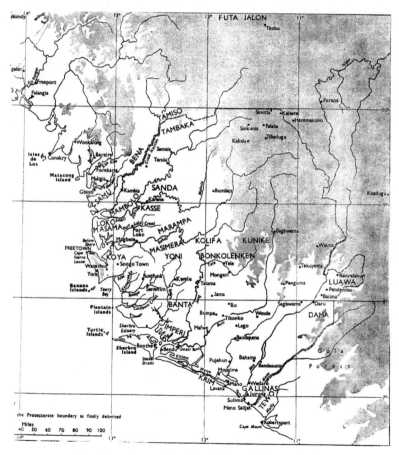

The Sierra Leone Coast in the early Nineteenth Century—*Christopher Fyfe—Inheritance—pp110*

A Portuguese man named Alvise da Cada Mosto, who, although he had not traveled with Pedro da Cintra, had heard the stories told by da Cintras sailors. From these stories he describes the area like this. *From Cape Liedo (Cape Sierra Leone), there extends a large mountain for about fifty miles along the coast, all of which is very high and covered with tall verdant trees. About eight miles from the shore, there are three small islands, the largest of which does not exceed ten or twelve miles in circumference. This the sailors gave the name Saluzze (Banana Islands) and they named the mountain Serra Lyola—Lion Mountains, on account of the continual roaring of thunder on its summit which is always enveloped in clouds.(Goddard 1925).*

The French had initially claimed that they were the first Europeans to visit the area in 1364, but the Portuguese disputed this and won the argument. But the name Serra Lyola eventually became Sierra Leone, which is a mixture of Italian and Portuguese, since the Italians were also describing what they saw as they made the maps of the sixteenth century. *(Kup1961)*

In this period, the African kings had sole sovereignty over the Sierra Leone Coastal region, and had been trading with Arabs during the Trans-Sahara Trade. This trade brought both traders and sailors who were seeking ivory, salt, gold, gum and slaves among other things, in exchange for Arabian cloth, spices, and other foreign goods. The Trans-Sahara Trade, which used routes pointing northwards, was a booming trade and accounted for the spread of Islam into in-land Sierra Leone and later to the coast. *(Fyfe 1964)*

The Mane Invasion

The Manes, an inland group of various tribes, invaded the coastal people between 1540 and 1550. They had come up the coast in war canoes after conquering the Cape Mount country. Their arrival brought different waves of tribes, the Lokos, Mendes, Konos and Vai, who were warriors and traders. Some of them were skilled artists, who carved ivory and produced items such as spoons, salt cellars and knife handles. Their war chief Bai Farma, was the King of the Loko. *(Fyfe 1962)*

When they arrived, the Manes proceeded to take over Bullom country, either through conquest or sedition. The invasion eventually divided the country along the Sierra Leone River. The Susu, Yalinka and Limbas settled in points north of the river and the Vai, Kono, Kru, and Loko, joined the Temnes and Bulloms in points south of the river. The chiefs in the south, apportioned their part of the country into kingdoms, which were then ruled by Clans. Four Mane kingdoms were created. The first extended northwards from Tagrin, the second settled around Port Loko, the third, which was known as the Kingdom of Sierra Leone or Boure, ran south from the Sierra Leone Peninsular and merged with the fourth which was the Kingdom of Sherbro. The Manes in these four ruling kingdoms cemented their authority by marrying into existing influential families in the area. Each kingdom was divided into sections and governed by 'sub' or 'section' chiefs or by governors, whom their King had left behind to administer the lands. *(Kup 1975)*

The descendants of the Manes were known for their intelligence and ability to learn. They were also very skilled in making weapons and iron tools. In the Bullom language, the word 'mane' means 'landed gentry', 'upper class' or 'ruling class' and to this day it is believed that Bullom people still regard the Caulkers as Manes, and give them the respect which the Manes expected and received all those years ago. *Stephen Bar Thebin Caulker (Uncle Bart) Article*

Chief Ya Cumba, a Kono chief, and his clan were left to govern the Southern or Sherbro Kingdom. He was in all likelihood an ancestor of Yema Cumba (Senora Doll) who later became the mother of all Caulkers.

The Sherbro People

The Bulloms or Sherbros were one of the earliest tribes the European sailors encountered. They occupied the south western coast of Sierra Leone, from the Ribbi River south of the Freetown Peninsula, all the way down to about the Bum River. Their catchment area also included Sherbro island, the Turtle islands, the Banana and Plantain islands as well as inland parts, which included areas now known as Bo and Moyamba

Districts. They called themselves southern Bulloms, to differentiate themselves from another group also called Bulloms, who reside north of the Freetown peninsula. According to oral history, there was a time when the boundaries of Bullom extended north of the Sierra Leone River. That changed when the Manes arrived and established their various kingdoms. The northern Bulloms are now completely assimilated with the Temnes and Susus. *(Kup 1975)* For purposes of this book, the southern Bulloms will be referred to as Sherbros.

As coastal people, the sherbro people are primarily fishermen, farmers and traders. Fishing is done in canoes, using large nets. The fish is either eaten fresh or dried (smoked) for trade in the interior. Farming, their second occupation, is primarily non-mechanized, with primitive tools at best. They grow cassava and rice, with a few sweet potatoes, yams and cola nuts. Their most important crops are the oil palm from which they extract palm oil and nut oil, and the coconut palm. Palm oil, nut oil, coconut oil and coconuts are traded. *(Hall 1938)*

Given the influence of the early European missionaries, many sherbros are Christian, although many of their communities no longer have active churches. Today, it is not uncommon for 'church' to be conducted by the school teacher and attended mostly by some of the students. Islam is also a very prominent religion in the area and as is true in Sierra Leone as a whole, Christians and Moslems live together peaceably, and often intermarry.

They believe in a single God, called Hobatoke. He is the father of all people and earth is the mother. One belief, which is common among the sherbros is, that death does not separate one from one's relatives who have passed on. The spirits of the dead are around all the time and must never be forgotten. The memory of the ancestors should not be neglected, as they are believed to provide protection and guidance, and by their intercession with Hobatoke, they can further the interests of the living. Hence they are honored during observances of the anniversaries of their death, holidays or community events. These ceremonies include an offering of cooked food, libations and feasts for the community. Individuals can also call on the ancestors by simply pouring a libation. *(Hall 1938)*

The Sherbro language which is spoken in the area, includes, European and other African words. It is not unusual to make out familiar sherbro words in Nigerian, Ghanaian, and other tribal languages, as well as some portuguese and other European words. For instance, the Portuguese word Mesa (table) is the same word used in Sherbro. The sherbro word 'Potho-nor' originally used to refer to the Portuguese, probably originated from the Portuguese Potho, but is now used in reference to all 'white people' and light skinned people. Because of their light complexion, the early Caulkers were thought of as white men or potho-nors and as the story goes, one of Thomas Corker's sons Robin (Skinner) was said to have been nicknamed 'the Old White man'.

Given their early exposure to Europeans, it is very likely that there were English speaking Sherbros well before the beginning of the colonial era. Until recently, Sherbros even had trouble speaking the Krio language—which today is the 'lingua-franca' of Sierra Leone. They either spoke, Sherbro, English or one of the other tribal languages, depending on their location. (Now, in post war Sierra Leone, Krio is more widely spoken).

The long association with the early Europeans enriched the Sherbros and created some cultural ideals and values which are similar to western culture, and different from that of the other tribes. The only other tribe or ethnic group, which is culturally similar to Europeans and Americans is the Krios. These are the descendants of the freed slaves who arrived from England, America and the Caribbean in the late 1700's.

During the colonial days, Sherbros and Krios formed a close alliance and began to intermarry from as far back as the 1870's, without any major problems. This close association of the Sherbros and the Krios gave the mistaken idea that, the Sherbros were Krios, but this is far from the truth.

The Poro Institution

In pre-colonial days the Sherbros were the most dominant tribal group in the area. Even before the arrival of the Europeans and the Manes, they had monarchies and administrative systems which were backed by strong cultural practices, some of which still exist today. One such cultural practice is the Poro Institution, which served as a check to the authority of the king or chief.

Poro is a very old institution which flourished first, among the Sherbros and then the Temnes. In the old days, it was much more powerful all over the country than it is today. Every town and village had a Poro bush in which their meetings and initiations were held. Initiations of new members lasted several months at the end of which, the initiates were each given a Poro name. Although initiations are still held today, the sessions are as short as two days, primarily due to school schedules.

In its hey day, those parts of the country which had Poro, were governed by the institution. Poro determined which fruits were picked and when, when fishing was to be done, and when villages were to be cleaned. When the Poro symbol was placed in the water, no one could fish until the fish had grown. When the symbol was placed on coconut trees, no one picked coconuts until they were ready for harvest. Decisions of peace, war or alliance were made by the Poro. In other words, Poro's influence was exercised in any situation where uniformity of action or co-operation was required. The penalty for disobeying a Poro order was death. In the old days, although a chief gave orders to individuals, the laws or general commands or prohibitions, could only be issued through Poro, since it was the only organ of public opinion. Today, the chief and tribal authorities appear to act independently of Poro, but the institution still plays an important role in the local administration, in those areas where it exists. *(Fyfe 1964)*

The word 'Poro' means 'One Word' or 'Unity'. This is the fundamental principle of the Institution. Poro, originally referred to as Belli-Paaro, (loosely translated as The core of Sherbro Society and Tradition), is described as a society of Peace. In his book "Sierra Leone Inheritance" Fyfe begins his description of Poro with these words.:—*"They say that it is a death, a resurrection and incorporation in the assembly of spirits or souls, with whom the members appear in the bush and help to eat the sacrifice which has been prepared for the spirits. But this is kept secret from the women and non members."* (Fyfe 1964, p 35)

In 1788, John Newton, then a slave trader, described the Poro Institution like this:

> "The Poro has both the legislative and executive authority and under their sanction, there is a police exercise which is by no means

> contemptible. Every thing belonging to the Poro, is mysterious and severe, but upon the whole, it has very good effects: and as any man, whether bond or free, who will submit to be initiated into their mysteries, may be admitted into the Order, it is a kind of common-wealth. Perhaps few people enjoy a more, simple, political freedom, than the inhabitants of Sherbro, belonging to the Poro (who are not slaves) further than they are bound by their own institutions. Private property is tolerably well secured and violence is much suppressed. It is an excellent institution which secured its members a high degree of political freedom." (Fyfe 1964, p100)

It is believed that a Poro member has access to every part of the country, while a non-Poro member is limited as to where he can go.

When the Poro is active in a location, women and all non-members must go indoors and clap until the 'all clear' is sounded.

The Rev.Dr William Fitzjohn, (a Caulker descendant) writes this about the Poro society:

> "Our people of Sierra Leone, particularly in the Protectorate, sought to preserve their culture by passing to each generation the things that its society had endeavored to maintain. They have been able to carry over their culture, chiefly through secret societies or initiation ceremonies. These societies and ceremonies acquired their unique manner of educating youth into the conscious privileges of adult life. These societies throughout their long histories have been the agencies for the village way of life. These societies are guardians not only of the traditional laws and ethical standards of tribal life, but also of the skills and knowledge necessary to make life functional. One of these, the Poro, imbues the young with the spirit of kinship to the tribe: New patterns of thought and skills are developed as our youth participate fully in the society of which they are part.
>
> In the Bondo society, (the secret society for women) the girls are instructed in the tribal qualities of womanhood and wifehood, in the domestic economy, dancing, singing, midwifery, nursing, fishing and in every tribal religious rite that concerns women". (Fitzjohn 1975)

Sir Milton Margai (the first Prime Minister of Sierra Leone) says, *"These secret societies exert a very great influence in the lives of protectorate natives. In the pre-protectorate days, they were the only medium for propagating essential knowledge among the people: and the female society the Bondo, still wields unassailable influence throughout the country."* All these fundamental practices grew out of the basic needs of a people. (*Fitzjohn 1975*)

Naming the children

The Sherbros name their children according to their position at birth. Hence the first boy is named Cho, and subsequent boys in the family are Thong, Sorba, Baki, and Raka etc. When a boy enters the Poro society, he receives a poro name and gives up his birth or 'baby' name. Similarly, girls are also named according to their birth position. Hence Boeh is the first girl, then Yema, Kona, Maheni, Chorkor etc. If there are two people in the family with the same birth position, i.e. two Konas,—a good possibility in polygamous families, or in a family where a mother and daughter have the same birth position, an addition is made to the baby's name. For instance, in my family, my mother, even though she was not Sherbro was considered a Kona according to her birth position of third girl in her family. So when a third daughter was born into our family, the baby was named Kona Ton Ton—Little Kona, differentiating her from her mother. Additional names are also given to differentiate similar names in the extended family. So there may be Boeh-Lesana, who is a different person from Boeh Tilang or Yemata (small Yema), who is different from Yema Lizzie (whose Christian name is Elizabeth) and so on.

More Europeans arrive

After the Mane invasion, the country settled down, and the area between the Sierra Leone River in the north and Cape Mount in the south was peaceful. For at least the next fifty years, all signs of war disappeared, or so it seemed. But by the middle of the 1600's however, 200 years after the Portuguese first arrived, more Europeans came to trade, and the existing ruling system of the Manes began to disintegrate. The chiefs fought each other for trade routes and waged war with anyone who refused to pay their customs taxes. Life on the coast changed. Indeed, life all over Africa changed with the onslaught of the Europeans, who proceeded to carve the continent into little parcels of land which they could rule. Boundaries which sometimes ran through villages, were established in order to mark which European country had claim to what area and over which people.

The African Rulers

Those who carried the title of 'king' or chief, still had some controlling influence, but their power was limited. Many of them dressed like the Europeans, in coats and trousers, and sometimes friendly ship's captains took them to visit England. They lived by trade, received gifts from their people and revenue from their 'strangers'. They enforced laws of trade, which forbade the sale of European salt, in order to protect local salt makers.

By the end of the 19th century, the African rulers began to lose some of their power. Some of those who had been 'Kings' were now known as 'Chiefs'. (It is suggested by some historians, that the title of 'King' was changed to 'Chief' so that the indigenous African leaders would not be perceived as being on the same level as Queen Victoria of England). *(Fyfe 1964)*

The Afro-Europeans

By the middle of the 1600's, two new cultural groups had appeared in Sierra Leone.—The Afro-Portuguese, descendants of the Portuguese traders, who had been there since the late 1400's, and the Afro-British, descendants of the British traders who arrived in the mid 1600's. By the late 1600's the Portuguese had left Sierra Leone, leaving behind their Portuguese/African descendants, who had control of the slave trade on Bunce Island. *(Kup 1975)*

Very few Afro-Portuguese were living on the southern coastal area where the Afro-British were settled. They mainly lived in the northern Temne towns. They were not chiefs, so they had little over-all power. They mainly traded was in slaves whom they obtained from the north. Known for their cruelty, their racial prejudice and unscrupulousness, no one liked the Afro-Portuguese. The European traders in particular, did not like them because they charged more money for their goods than the Africans traders. They did not farm or hunt, because the chiefs refused to give them land for agriculture. Instead they acted as the middlemen in any trading activity, but unlike the Afro-British, they were not supported militarily by European trading companies, which possessed armed ships. *(Kup 1975)*

The Afro-British on the other hand, were the descendants of the British traders, and generally worked for the Royal African Company. Men like, Thomas Corker *(later spelled Caulker)* William Clevland *(later spelled Cleveland)*, Zachary Rogers and John Tucker, all worked for the company and had African wives. Rogers and Tucker worked for the Gambia Adventures. The local story about the relationship between Corker, Rogers and Tucker, was that they were three cousins who had come to trade in Sierra Leone. It is more likely however, that they became related by marriage since their wives (many of whom were Caulker women) were very likely related and had been given to them as gifts, by the Chief. *(Fyfe 1964)*

All new agents who arrived in the area, were required to get permission from the King or Chief, if they wanted to trade in his chiefdom. This involved 'putting Kola'—(*a formality which entails bringing gifts and/ or money, as part of the price for the privilege of trading.*) After receiving the 'Kola' the Chief then agreed to the proposal, in return for regular payments of gifts or maybe a commission on sales. With this agreement, the Chief provided the land on which the agent could build his business, and became the agent's landlord. As landlord, the Chief was responsible for the agent's safety, for upholding the agent's interests, and for anything the agent did which was wrong. It was also not unusual for a Chief to give the gift of one of the women in his chiefdom, or even one of his daughters to his guest, especially if he liked that guest—(A custom which was a testament to African hospitality.) So Thomas Corker married into the Ya Cumba family, who were the rulers of the 'Old Kagbor Chiefdom,' which included the Plantain Islands. John Tucker's descendants settled on the Sherbro Island and became quite influential as chiefs. Zachary Rogers the chief agent, married into a Sherbro household on the southern part of the coast. Between 1677 and 1681, two Rogers' sons married the daughters of King Siaka, of the Massaquoi ruling family, which ruled the area of Cape Mount. They founded a dynasty, and became known as the Massaquois. William Clevland, who came later, settled on Banana Island. He married Kate Corker (daughter of Robin (Skinner) Caulker, grand daughter of Thomas and Senora Doll), and wielded a lot of influence on the island (*Kup 1975*)

Within two generations, the Afro-British had become rich and had built their own towns with the help of the company slaves who worked for them. It was easy for the agents to use their positions in the company to get the goods which some believe may have been stolen from their employers, which they used to bargain for the land on which they established their plantations. (*Fyfe 1964*)

Chapter II

The European Ancestors

The Ancient Corkers

One cannot tell the story of the Caulkers of Sierra Leone, without examining the origins of Thomas Corker, the first Corker who came to Sierra Leone.

Our story begins with a James Corker of the parish of Wragby, in Huntwick, Yorkshire, England. He lived in the mid-1500s and had seven sons. One of them, Francis, was born in 1560. Francis also had seven sons and one of them by a second marriage was Edward Corker (E.Louise, 2001)

Edward Corker who lived in Ireland, was the Registrar of the Chancery in Dublin. He was the first recipient of the Coat of Arms in 1696. His son Thomas, born in 1653, grew up to become a physician, and worked as a ship's doctor. During one of Dr. Corker's journeys, the ship landed in Falmouth, a port in Cornwall, England. There he met and fell in love with a local girl named Jane Newman. They were married on April 25th 1666 and settled in Falmouth. They had four children.—Robert (Jan 29th 1667), Thomas jr. (February 4th 1669), and two daughters, Jane and Anne. The children's baptismal certificates can be seen today in the Falmouth parish records of the church of St. Charles the Martyr, and their last name is listed as Calker instead of Corker.

Dr. Thomas Corker died in 1680, when his children were very young—(Robert was 13 years old and Thomas jr. was only 11 years old).

They were raised by their mother's brother, John Newman who was a lawyer. Robert, grew up to become the Receiver-General of His Royal Highness the Prince of Wales in 1709 and was given the honor again in 1731. He was a member of parliament in 1721 and 1728, and Mayor of Falmouth five times. These achievements clearly showed his 'Corker' leadership traits. But although he acquired large holdings of property during his lifetime, by the time he died in 1730, Robert owed large sums of money. (E. Louise 2001)

The question often asked in Sierra Leone—*"Have you ever seen a wealthy Caulker?"* seems to have been true even then. His younger brother Thomas, whose story will be told later, went to sea.

Origin of the family Name by Stephen Bar Thebin Caulker

"Over the years, there has been a certain degree of confusion about the name Corker or Caulker, among the Bullom or Sherbro speaking people, along the coast of Sierra Leone. Depending on the voice inflection in sherbro, the word caulker can mean 'a shoe', or many other things. I once heard a sherbro speaking lady who, when asked if she too was a Caulker, replied, "No! Do you ever see me wearing shoes"?

For a long time we Caulkers in Sierra Leone presumed that we had that surname, either because our ancestors caulked boats, or (as the sherbros believed) wore shoes, because of our English parentage.

I first came across the name spelt as 'Corcor' in Ireland, when it appeared as an alias on Edward Corker's confirmation record of the family coat of arms in 1666. From Journals of the Irish Memorials Association, "Corcor" also appears sometimes as the sole family name.

'Cor' is the Latin word for heart, thus 'Cor Cor' literally means 'Heart Heart'. It appears on the top of the shield of the family coat of arms. This top part is also regarded as the family crest, and is the family good luck charm. This suggests that the original name was 'Corcor'. I suspect that the family may have been of Viking origin and they either came to Britain via France with William the Conqueror in 1066 or later, when the Vikings invaded and settled in Cornwall and Ireland in large numbers. There are records of a Richard Corcor who

lived at 'Cor Castle' in County Cork, Ireland. He died in Ireland on the 6th of March 1873 at age 28.

In 1987 when I started my research into the pre-Sierra Leone and European roots of our 'Caulker Family', my family and I visited Falmouth in Cornwall, United Kingdom. We saw the Memorial Stone which was erected in memory of our ancestor Thomas Corker, in the Parish Church, St Charles the Martyr, where he had been baptized and was buried.

All the documents I was able to obtain—his parent's marriage certificate, and their sons, Thomas and Robert's baptismal certificates, had the family name spelled 'Calker'. In those days, in the seventeenth century, the spellings of family names were not standardized. By the end of the 1800s, in Sierra Leone, the spelling of Corker had changed to Caulker. Regardless of the spelling which is used in the records, the common and uniting factor was the Coat-of-Arms and it appeared even on ancient grave stones in Ireland, and sometimes even on unmarked graves.

The Corker/Caulker Coat of Arms

During the Middle Ages in Europe, owning a coat-of-arms, was a way of identifying prominent families and warriors, especially when they went to war. When men went to war, the crest was given to them, often embroidered on a scarf by a sweetheart. This was to bring good luck. But the flag which they carried, showed the full Coat of Arms.

The Corker family coat of arms has been in existence since the middle ages and has been described as ancient Corker, alias CorCor heraldic. The Duchal Crest is located at the top and is composed of a single crowned red heart, which rests on a cloth ring between two laurel leaves. The whole thing appears to be sitting on top of a helmet above the shield which shows a lion, rearing on the left leg with the forelegs elevated, the right leg above the left, and the head in profile. The family motto **Sacrificium Deo Cor Contritum,**—Latin for—"My contrite heart is a sacrifice to God."—Psalm 51 verse 17. is etched on the bottom of the Coat of Arms."

Caulker/Corker Coat of Arms

There have been two confirmations of the family coat of arms over the years. The first was granted to **Edward Corker** of Ireland during the reign of King William III of England, Scotland, France and Ireland. He had to plead for, and won a confirmation of the Corker Arms in 1696. The Edward Corker coat of Arms carries a blue lion.

In 1981, **Stephen Bar Thebin Caulker** of the House of Mambo, Kagboro Chiefdom, Sierra Leone, West Africa, was the second to be awarded a certificate of confirmation, after he had done extensive research to prove that he was descended from the Corker/Caulker family which had carried the original coat of arms. The lion in this case is black, indicating that Stephen Bar Thebin Caulker is a black man.—A Caulker from Sierra Leone. In the year 2000, Stephen Bar Thebin Caulker granted permission to the Caulker Descendants of Sierra Leone, to use the coat of arms as their emblem.

The Coat of Arms was not the only commonality between the Corkers of England and Ireland and the Caulkers of Sierra Leone. It is also interesting to note that the first names used in the 1500s, such as James, Thomas, Robert, Kate, Stephen, Charles, Richard, John, Francis and William, are still commonly used today by the present day Caulkers of Sierra Leone. (*E.Louise, 2001)*

Women did not wear the coat of arms, as they did not go to war. They only wore the crest. The picture below shows the graves of George and Lulu Caulker of Mambo House, erected by their son Stephen Bar Thebin Caulker. The grave on the left, Lulu (wife of George), has a crest, whilst the grave on the right, has the full coat of arms. Both of these grave stones can be seen in the village of Mambo, Kagboro chiefdom, where George and Lulu lived.

Grave stones of George and Lulu Caulker at Mambo

Part II

The Caulkers of Sierra Leone

Chapter III

Thomas Corker and Senora Doll

Young Thomas Corker grew up in a port city, where ships arrived daily from different parts of the world. He became fascinated by the sea and loved to listen to the stories of riches—Gold from the Gold coast, Ivory from the Ivory Coast, Gum, Grain, timber and slaves from the Rice Coast, on the West African Coast—which the sailors brought back. He was so determined to seek the adventure and excitement which he had heard of on the wharfs of Portsmouth, that at a young age, (13 or 14) he went to sea probably working as a cabin boy at first. In 1684, at age fifteen, he got a job with the Royal African Company.

The Royal African Company

By the middle of the fifteenth century, several English and Dutch companies had been formed and had been given charters to trade on the West African Coast. By 1618, England had also established regular trade on Africa's west coast, and that year, granted a charter to the Company of Adventurers of London, which had already been trading in Africa. But the company was not granted the right to trade on the Sherbro River until 1651. In 1672, the Adventurers of London were succeeded by the Royal African Company which already had a factory in Jamaica Town, on the Sierra Leone river. Here they collected elephant's teeth (Ivory), bees wax, cowhides and slaves. The R.A.C also sent ships to the Sherbro River to trade for red-wood timber, which was used for making dyes.

Thomas Corker arrived in Sierra Leone in 1684, as an employee of the Royal African Company and was stationed for a couple of years in 'the rivers' (on the mainland). By tradition, on his arrival he had to present himself to the King of the area. The King at the time was of the Ya Cumba family—the ruling family on the coast of the Yawry Bay. Coming from Europe, and being a staff member of the Royal African Company, Thomas was considered a stranger in a high position. As was customary, King Ya Cumba gave his daughter Yema, (Yema means second born daughter) who was known by the Europeans as Senora Doll, in marriage to this stranger whom he liked.

Young Thomas and Yema (Senora Doll) were married, probably according to the customary or native law. In 1685, their first son Stephen, was born and he was followed by Robin also known as Skinner in 1687. The local children nicknamed Skinner, 'the old white man', because he was so light-skinned. (*To most Africans, when a person is light-skinned, s/he is called 'white man' or 'potho.' Even today, when an African has been overseas for a long time and returns home with western ideas and or western behaviors, s/he is considered to have become 'potho' or 'white man'.*)

Thomas and Senora Doll sent their sons to school in Liverpool, England. When they returned home, like many of the other boys who had been sent abroad, they were employed in their father's company. The company management was not happy with the idea of hiring "these African-European children" (called mulattos), but Agent Corker was able to convince his bosses that African children of mixed parentage were a good investment and were necessary because:

a. They could communicate with the white man and act as translators in business transactions.
b. They knew the white man's language and his ways of doing business, which was an advantage.
c. There were certain jobs at the factory which needed to be done, but which the white traders did not want to do. The mulattos were

more than willing to do these jobs, like carpentry, blacksmithing and storekeeping.

Agent Corker's final argument was:

d. The African relatives of these mulatto boys were more willing to do business through them, because they trusted them much more than they trusted the white traders.

And so the young employees were allowed to continue working with the company. *(Fyfe 1964)*

Indeed, trust was an issue between the Europeans and the Africans. John Newton, who at the time was a slave trader, had this to say about the level of suspicion which existed between the Africans and the white men.—*"With a few exceptions, the English and Africans consider each other as consummate villains who are always watching for opportunities to do mischief. In short, we have, I fear too deservedly, a very unfavorable character upon the coast. When I have charged a black with unfairness and dishonesty, he has answered, if able to clear himself, with an air of disdain, "What! Do you think I am a white man?"* (Fyfe, p74,1964)

In 1692, Thomas Corker was promoted to the position of Chief Agent for the RAC, and was based on York island, which is located between the island of Sherbro and the main land. The European community on the island was large, and most of the agents had African wives. Corker's letter of appointment follows below. It is presented exactly as it was written in those days, so the English may seem a bit strange.

"London the 27th of September 1692
Agent Thomas Corker

At the instance of your Brother and other friends here with the good Character wee have from people coming from thence, of your diligence and good behavior in the Station you have acted hitherto, wee have chosen you in the roome of Agent Henry Gibson, to be our Chiefe at Yorke Island Sierra Leone and places adjacent at the sallary of 100 pounds sterling per annum. And accordingly, wee have consigned to you the goods, provisions etc upon the Anne Capt John Leech as by the bills of lading and invoices enclosed import 2,897 pounds, 8 shillings and 8 pence wherein we have been careful to send nothing but what our predecessors and others have advised to be proper. Upon arrival of the ship, (which we pray God to send safe) be diligent to receive the goods and dispose of them with what expedition you can to make us returns by the ship. You will find the cargoes suited for the trade of Sherbro and Sierra Leone etc. And for your assistance, we have chosen Mr. Charles Eaton to be your Second who takes his passage upon the Ship Anne."

It ends with the paragraph:

> "Robert Gun hath been very forward to encourage interlopers and privateers very much to our damage though wee have been the means to promote him to what he is. Wee therefore order you to show him no countenance by employing him untill you can bring him to espouse our interest against all other people which you may the more easily do business with if you take the pains to buy among the natives yourself.
>
> We rest,
> Your loving friends . . ." (Fyfe, p63 1964)

In 1698, Thomas was once again promoted, this time, to the position of Governor for the RAC in the Gambia. He was stationed on an island called James Island where the British had built a fort (Fort James), and had hoisted the Union Jack (the British flag) for the first time on African soil in 1664. (E. Louise 2001)

The Royal African Company which had been doing business on James Island since 1672, was having problems with the French, who had bombarded their Fort and destroyed it. In 1697, the year before Thomas Corker's appointment as governor, a treaty was signed with the French and the Island was returned to the RAC. When Thomas arrived in the Gambia, he immediately went to work establishing new factories up the river Gambia and on the coast of Guala. He refused to give the French the right to trade, beyond James Island. When they paid no attention to his ruling, Thomas gave orders to his crew to fire on their boats. On April 12th 1700, a French trader, Mr. Andre De Brue decided to visit Thomas to discuss the problems, which centered around the rights of the French to trade in British territories. Unfortunately at the time, Thomas was having an attack of gout, and sent a message to Mr. De Brue, saying that he could not see him that day. But De Brue came anyway. Unfortunately because of the gout Governor Corker, who had been determined to receive him in full regalia, could not do so. Although he was dressed in his full uniform, he had to wear slippers. Never the less, he and De Brue seemed to have had a great time together. They ate and drank till late that night, but settled nothing. On a later date, Thomas returned De Brue's visit, and once again they spent the time eating and drinking, and doing little to resolve their dispute. *(Fyfe 1993)*

But although Thomas Corker had been very successful in his work, there were those who were determined to bring him down. It was not too long before charges were being brought against him. One charge was that he had brought rioters from Sherbro to the Gambia to disrupt the operations there.

By the mid 1700, shortly after his meeting with Mr. Debrue the French trader, the company relieved Thomas Corker of his duties and called him home to answer to these charges of wrong doings. He left Sierra Leone as ordered, and landed in Falmouth in July 1700. There, the press reported that he had brought home 45 ounces of gold, several black slaves, elephant's teeth (Ivory), and hides among other things.

The authorities were never able to prove anything against him. But his health had begun to fail around the end of his term as governor anyway, and he was a sick man by the time he arrived in England. On September 10th 1700, two months after his arrival in Falmouth, Thomas Corker died from malaria and heart problems, at the age of thirty one. *(Fyfe 1993)*

His brother Robert erected a marble monument in his memory in the Church of St. Charles the Martyr, where he was baptized. The memorial stone is the oldest in the church and is still very prominent. The words on the memorial are written in Latin but the church added a translated plaque.

THE CAULKERS OF SIERRA LEONE

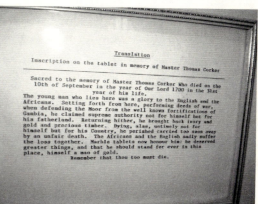

The Thomas Corker Memorial Monument, with translation, seen at the Church of St.Charles the Martyr, Falmouth, England.

"Sacred to the memory of Master Thomas Corker who died on the 10th of September in the year of our Lord 1700, in the 31st year of his life. The young man who lies here was a glory to the English and the Africans. Setting forth from here performing deeds of war, when defending the Moors from the well known fortifications of Gambia. He claimed supreme authority not for himself, but for his fatherland.

Returning hither, he brought back Ivory and gold and precious timber. Dying, alas, untimely not for himself, but for his country, he perished, carried too soon away by unfair death. The Africans and the English sadly suffer the loss together. Marble tablets now honor him: he deserved greater things, and that he should stand for ever in this place, himself a man of gold. Remember that thou too must die."

At some point after Thomas Corker's death, the Royal African Company began having trouble with the Dutch and private traders who were also taking slaves from Sierra Leone to the plantations in the West Indies. This conflict seriously affected their trade on Bunce Island and in 1728, some of the Afro-Portuguese managers on the island led a revolt which eventually caused the R.A.C to abandon their fort on Bunce Island and their factory in Jamaica Town on the Sherbro river. By 1750, the Royal African Company lost its charter and had to close down its operations. (*Goddard,1925*)

Local history suggests that, after her husband's death, Senora Doll, (Yema Cumba) very likely stood for the chieftaincy elections and won, thus succeeding her father as ruler. She was known as Queen of Tasso or Queen of Yawry Bay. As Queen she was a powerful figure, who wielded a lot of influence in the affairs of the chiefdom before she died. During her rule she participated in trade and was able to obtain European goods which she liked. She is said to have been fond of silk stockings, silk handkerchiefs and linen fabrics, and received bright colored chintz fabric from England, which she used to make her clothes. Her cultural and living standards, it is said, could be compared with any middle to upper class English person of her time. (*E.Louise 2001*)

She lived for 22 years after her husband's death. Her sons Stephen and Robin, kept their paternal surname—Corker, and inherited their claim to rule, from her. After her death, her oldest son Stephen Corker, then 37 years old, was crowned King of Kagbor.

The Corker/Caulkers used their European heritage and connections to expand their kingdom and to further their trading exploits. From the 1700s onward, Corker girls married prominent European and Afro-European traders such as the Rogers Tuckers and Clevelands, and produced new Afro-European clans. These clans, it is said, became the most notorious Afro-European slave traders in the 18th century. Around this time, the spelling of their name changed to CAULKER, more than likely because of the way the Bulloms pronounced CORKER. And so, through trade, marriage and strong African and European ties the Corkers now known as Caulkers became very powerful.

Chapter IV

Legends and Stories of the Old Kagbor Chiefdom

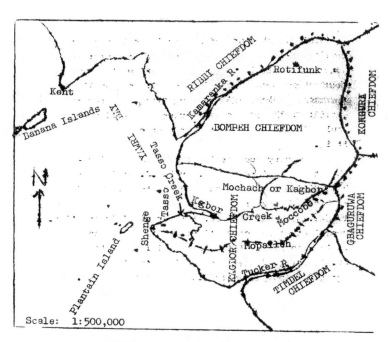

Map showing Old and Present KAGBOR

—— Chiefdom Boundaries
∙∙∙∙ Old Kagbor
—•—+ Motor Road

Map showing Old and Present KAGBOR from 'A short story of the Kagbor Chiefdom'—Lionel Tower (1984)

Key:—Chiefdom Boundaries _____ Old Kagbor . . . Motor Road . . . / . . . / . . . /

Before we move forward with the story of the Caulkers, let us take a step back and try to understand how and why the present chiefdoms came to be as they are today. This is a story told by a local teacher, Mr. Lionel Tower, who, in a small unpublished book, 'Old Kagbor', written around 1984 describes the old chiefdom of Kagbor using stories he was told by the elders, by those who witnessed events, and from his own experiences.

How the chiefdom got its name.

Kagbor must have acquired its name from the Kagbor River which runs through it, or from a small village known as Mocharch. As the story says, the village of Mocharch was difficult to reach by boat and it took hard paddling upstream to get there. The river was therefore called LA KA GBOH, meaning "paddling to the village is difficult". Other stories say that it was a place where a powerful female chief, the wife of a hunter named Gbana Banda had an egg plant (locally known as garden eggs) farm. The Sherbro word for egg plant is ngboh, and the place was called KA NGBOH—the place of garden eggs. Regardless of the origin of the name, the whole area was called Kagbor.

The story of the two Ruling Houses

According to the legend, a group of hunters from the Mane group, with their Kono leader, Ya Cumba had been chasing an elephant for several weeks, but could not catch it. So they decided to rest. They arrived at a place on high ground, which lay between two streams near the Yawry bay, known as the Suhs and Barka streams. Here a huge cave-rock, hung over the river. The area was, and still is a beautiful and peaceful location, with a magnificent view of the Yawry Bay and the Atlantic ocean. The hunters were so tired that their leader said, "Tasso" which in the Kono language means, "Let us rest here." So they rested and the villagers, always hospitable, took care of them. The hunters loved this location and were so content they decided to stay. They were given permission to build huts and marry the village women. Meanwhile, their fellow tribesmen who were concerned because they had not heard from the hunting party for a very long time, sent out a search party. Eventually the 'lost' hunters were found. When the rescue party saw their new location, they too fell in love with it and decided to stay. As the population grew, the village expanded and a new town named Tasso was born. It became the seat of the ruling chief

The second ruling house

At about the same time these hunters arrived at the place now called Tasso, another group of Mane hunters, set out on their hunting spree. This time their quest for elephants took them in a different direction, further inland and up river. Their leader was known as Gbana Banda from Banta. This group also found a place to rest and like the group at Tasso, they decided to settle where they had stopped to rest. They named their village Mocharch.

As the legend goes, over time pieces of rags and charcoal wood which had been thrown into the river from Tasso, slowly drifted upstream and were noticed by the people in Mocharch. They were puzzled and decided to investigate. They traveled by canoe, and followed the stream, to the mouth of the river, where they noticed smoke. They followed the smoke until they arrived at the village of Tasso. There they paid homage to the leader Ya-Cumba, and greeted their fellow hunters, who entertained, them. After spending several days during which they had a good time with food and drink, they returned home to Mocharch. Many years later, Mocharch was destroyed, and the village was moved to a new location called Mocobo. Today, Mocobo is the seat of the Sosant Dick house.

It is not surprising that both groups claimed to have arrived and settled in the area first.

For expediency, these two houses have been named House A—the Cumba-Caulker House, whose original seat of government was on Tasso, and House B, the Dyehbo Sosant Dick House whose seat of government began in Mocharch, and later moved to Mocobo. According to the history Yema Cumba, a descendant of Chief Ya Cumba, who married Thomas Corker, inherited the Tasso chieftaincy. After her death the Cumba-Caulker House came into being and Tasso became their first seat of chiefdom. The Cumba-Caulker house was the only ruling house in the area, recognized by the colonial government. The Sosant Dick (Bono Dick) House—House B, was not recognized as a ruling house until many, many, years later, after the Protectorate was formed in 1896.

Old Kagbor Chiefdom

Originally, the chiefdom encompassed only the Tasso area but it gradually expanded to include a greater part of the main land and the Plantain and Banana Islands. Old Kagbor Chiefdom was bounded by the Kamaranka River which is now the boundary between Ribbi and Bompeh on the north, the Tucker River on the south, the Gbaguruwa and Kokbura Chiefdoms on the east, and the Banana islands near Kent, the Plantain Islands near Shenge, the mainland near the Yawri Bay and the Atlantic Ocean on the west.

It extended approximately thirty two miles from east to west and 30 miles from north to south—an area of roughly nine hundred and sixty (960) square miles. Today this area is made up of two chiefdoms—Bompeh and Kagboro. While it was originally purely Sherbro, today it is a mix of several tribes—Sherbros, Mendes, Temnes, Fullahs, and Susus. The whole area was initially called Greater Kagbor or the Bompeh Kingdom.

For a long time Tasso was the burial place of the Caulkers. Now the old cemetery, which has the Mausoleums of the ancient Caulkers, is currently under the control of the Poro Society, which also controls access to it. No non-Poro member is allowed to go there. This writer has been told that trying to do so without permission from the Poro Society, incurs the death penalty. The Cave rock at Tasso still exists and it is still a place where sacred ceremonies are performed. When a new chief is crowned, he is required to go to Tasso for a sacred ceremony. (A female chief must send a representative who is a member of the Poro Society to represent her at the ceremony, since women are not allowed there.) The Bompeh Caulkers stopped burying their chiefs at Tasso, when the Sosant Dick House, the second ruling house, began its rule in 1909, and the chiefdom headquarters was briefly moved to Mocobo.

The story of Plantain Island.

Plantain Island was named after a slave dealer and pirate called John Plantain, who settled there from 1700 to 1720. At the time, the area known as Plantain, was made up of the Main Land, Plantain Island and two smaller islands which lay behind the main island. Apparently this was a strategic location to the Yawri Bay, the Sherbro River and Tucker's peninsular. John Plantain stayed on the island for twenty years and became wealthy from the slave trade. In 1720 he left the island to settle in Madagascar, an island off the east coast of South Africa. After his departure, other slave dealers and pirates like John Hawkins and John Newton, who at the time was his employee, came to settle on the island. The island was a significant location during the slave trade, having been commandeered by the slave traders, for its strategic location.

When chief Charles Caulker (great grandson of Thomas and Senora Doll) became chief in 1780, he ruled 'The old Kagbor Chiefdom. But he moved from Tasso and settled on Plantain island, making it his headquarters. Unfortunately he was beheaded by the Clevelands in 1785 and was replaced by his brother William. Through all the family squabbles of the time, Plantain remained the chief's residence until it was destroyed during the Caulker wars of the mid 1840s.

Life on the island was simple. While the men engaged in fishing, the women did gardening and grew different crops. One very prolific crop was Egusi (melon seeds used for cooking) called Nsanga in Sherbro. The island was therefore referred to as Yel Nsagna-Egusie Island. Although the name 'Plantain' is still the more commonly used name, it is still referred to by some of the locals as Yel Nsanga.

Today, with erosion, the slave pen has been cut off from the main island, (as shown in picture below), and Plantain island is just a shadow of itself.

During the Hut Tax War of 1898, Plantain Island was a place of refuge for the people of Shenge, but in 1933 Temnes and other tribes started arriving and settling on the island.

Plantain Island in 2007

Division of The Old Kagbor Chiefdom.

When chief Stephen Caulker of Old Kagbor died in 1810, by custom, his brother Thomas Kon Tham succeeded him. Just at that time, Stephen's son George Stephen Caulker (also called Ba Charch), had returned from school in England and was employed as a storekeeper by a Jewish trader named Nathan Isaacs. While George was in England, he had learned the English rules which allowed the oldest child, to rule. So after his uncle Thomas Kon Tham was crowned, he begged the new chief to let him rule part of the chiefdom. Thomas Kon Tham agreed, and gave George a small area south of the Cockboro River which included the Plantain Island and Shenge, while he kept the Banana Islands and the northern mainland.

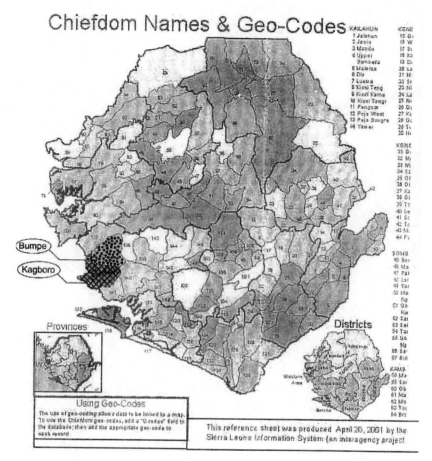

Dotted area showing modern day Bompeh and Kagboro Chiefdoms

George Stephen Caulker I (Bar Charch) and his brother Thomas Stephen (Bar Tham) who had also studied in England, made Plantain Island their base. Thomas Stephen, who had been working as a teacher for the Church Missionary Society, and was also translating hymns into the Sherbro language, opened a school on the island, taught English and also helped his brother to deal with matters of the new chiefdom.

Although the chiefdom was now divided, the Caulkers of Bompeh never forgot that they were from Old Kagbor. Since they were now occupying only a section of the "Mother Country, Kagbor" they named their Chiefdom Bompeh, which in sherbro means "a portion or section of the whole vast land." Remember that Kagbor had, for a long time, been regarded by the previous Caulker rulers as their home land and Tasso as their family headquarters. Therefore, when the Bompeh Caulkers wanted to initiate their male children into the Poro Secret Society, they still took them over to Tasso. They sent all their male children to be educated at the Rufus Clark and Wife Training School in Shenge. When any member of the Bompeh Caulker family died, the corpse was taken to Tasso for burial. All traditional and ceremonial affairs of Bompeh were done at Tasso. In about 1915 however, when the ruling chief, Madam Sophia Neale Caulker was deposed by the colonial authorities and the chieftaincy was handed over to the Mocobo House,—the second ruling house in Kagbor, the Caulkers of Bompeh cut off their connection with the Shenge Plantain Caulkers because they did not wish to recognize or pay allegiance to another ruling house in their homeland."

How Shenge acquired its name.

Shenge town, was initially known as Kai (ko), which means a place where salt is made, or the salt area. But in 1840, when chief Thomas Stephen established a Poro bush there it became Shenge ko.

As the story goes, in the past, many of the men in the Bompeh chiefdom, including the Caulker chiefs, were Poro members while the Caulker chiefs of Plantain and Shenge were not. But after his experience with the Poro members in Bompeh, Thomas Stephen was determined to have a meeting place for members of the Poro Society right in Shenge, because Tasso, the traditional Poro bush was far away from his headquarters on Plantain Island. He decided to make Shenge the sub "Fai"(Poro bush), where ceremonies could be performed. Today ceremonies are still performed at this site.

Regardless of where a Poro bush is located, there are laws for its members and non-members and there is punishment for disobeying those laws. For instance, a woman is strictly forbidden to become a member of the Poro Society and cannot interfere in society business in any way. Today, if a woman tries to interfere in Poro business, she simply disappears and is not heard of again. Well, as the story goes, one day, a woman who was curious about how the society operated at the Shenge

Fai went in the bush to spy on them. She was caught, and taken into the bush—Fai Ko, where she was executed and her body was publicly displayed. A song was composed "Cheng-ke, O ya Cheng-ke, chen wei po'eh: chen-ke, cheng-ko? Interpreted means—Don't you see, Oh yah, are you not afraid, don't you see there? The word cheng-ke ko (don't you see there?) became familiar to the people, and the place became known as Cheng-ko, which is now anglicized to become Shenge-ko."(*Tower*).

When George Stephen died in 1831, his only surviving son, Thomas Kugba was too young to become chief, and his uncle Thomas Stephen became the Regent Chief, ostensibly to rule until Thomas Kugba came of age. The following year, (1832) Thomas Kon Tham of Bompeh, died and was succeeded by his younger brother Charles. Charles started opening the country to timber traders, as the trees on the banks of the Rokel, Port Loko and Melakovi rivers were almost exhausted, and new sites were needed. By the time Charles died in 1846, a lively timber trade had been established on the shores of the Yawry Bay. (*Tower*)

Chapter V

The Cleveland Connection

In the mid 1730's, thirty years after Thomas Corker's death, a slave ship was wrecked near the Banana Islands. On board the ship was the ship mate, William Clevland, a young Englishman who was the son of a Captain William Clevland of the Royal Navy, of Tapley, England. He was also the brother of the then Secretary of the Admiralty. *(E.Louise 2001)*

Young William sought refuge on the Banana Island, (one writer reports that Clevland actually left the slave ship in order to marry the daughter of one of the Corkers It is likely that Robin (Skinner) Corker, gave Clevland his daughter Kate as his wife, as was the custom, after Clevland had worked for him.) Clevland eventually settled on the island. *(Kup1975)*. After working for a few years and learning how to trade, Clevland began his own business and eventually went into slave trading.

William and Kate had two children, John, born in 1740 and Elizabeth, born in 1741. He also had another son named James, by a woman from the Kissi tribe named Ndamba. Like all the other traders, William sent his children to school in England and he himself made several trips to South Carolina in North America, probably bringing slaves to market. Some of these journeys were made with his daughter Elizabeth who often went to visit with their American Clevland relatives. When William died in 1758, his daughter Elizabeth was 17 and his son John was 18. He was buried on Bunce Island, where he had done his slave trading. *(E.Louise 2001)*.

Young John Clevland, who had been in school in England when his father William died, returned home to Banana Island to preside over the Clevland family business. He continued the family's slave trading business, as well as the ivory, gun, gold and turtle shell trade. When he died around 1764, he left behind two sons, James and William and a daughter Catherine. *(Kup`1975)*.

Following John's death, his half brother James, took over the family business, and took responsibility for his sister Elizabeth and the children. The two boys were sent to school in England and the daughter Catherine, then a young child of about 8 years old, was sent with her aunt Elizabeth to live in South Carolina. Due to her parentage, Elizabeth was very light skinned and could pass for a white woman. She became a permanent resident of South Carolina, and married a physician, Dr. William Hardcastle, who was a surgeon in the Royal Army. (*E. Louise 2001*). The couple raised Catherine as their own, and when Elizabeth died, her plantation, the Racoon Hill Plantation in South Carolina, was willed to Catherine. Catherine married a freed slave, Andrew Dibble and raised a family of her own. Their descendants are the Nauddin-Dibbles.

Meanwhile back in Africa, James Clevland, was living in luxury on the Banana Islands. It is said that his life style was as European as he could possibly make it. His house, which was built like a country house, (possibly meaning it was built like a local house), was furnished like an English house. It was difficult to know what his thoughts on any topic really were, for it is said that, when he was with white men, he was a white man and when he was with black men, he acted and spoke like a black man. *(Fyfe 1964)*

In spite of his wealth, it seems James had difficulty getting along with the Corkers. Although he liked their power and influence, he was envious and resented them for it. He became so obsessed by his quest for power, that he even used the name Corker instead of Clevland. One explanation for the name change could be that, although he was not Kate Corker's child, he was raised in the Corker/Clevland household and must have thought, if he carried the name Corker, he would be just as powerful as his cousins. He even joined the Poro Society, thinking that he could increase his local power. The Poro institution was and still is the 'sine qua non' of Sherbro society. It had control over the political, cultural, educational and religious life of the people. Hence for James, joining Poro in his quest for power was a prudent move.

In those days, (and the same may be true today), there were two ways to gain recognition and power in an area. The first was by going to **War,** since waging war was a sure way of acquiring sovereignty if one was victorious. The second was by **Trading**.

So it was that as James' obsession grew worse, he broke his ties with the Corkers and chose the first option. A ferocious war began, between the Clevlands and the Caulkers in 1785 when James sent a force headed by Bemba (Lord North, as he called himself) a Clevland employee, to Plantain Island, where the Corker chief resided. Bemba was able to surprise and behead Chief Charles Corker. After this deed was accomplished, James compensated Bemba well by giving him land at Cape Shilling and promoting him to the position of Head Man. In his new position, Bemba sold many free men and head men into slavery and became very powerful. The resulting war was a boon to the slave traders, who loved this turn of events, because it created lots of war prisoners who could be purchased (*Fyfe 1964*)

The Cleveland/ Caulker Wars

Bent on success, James also decided that it would be to his advantage if he married a Corker wife. So he married one of the late chief's sisters. This of course did nothing to help his relationship with the Corkers, and much to his frustration, it did not give him the level of power he craved. He continued to rule the Banana Islands until his death in 1791 when his nephew, William succeeded him. (*Fyfe 1964*).

Meanwhile, the late Chief's brothers, William and Stephen Corker, were constantly quarrelling, because they could not agree on which one of them was to avenge their brother. William, who had now succeeded his brother Charles, did nothing about avenging his brother's murder during his five year rule. He died in 1797 and Stephen, who was crowned chief in 1798, immediately began making plans to attack the Clevlands.

Young William Cleveland, (*It is not clear when the spelling of Clevland changed to Cleveland*) was thought to be a lazy and easy going man, but he was able to keep the family trading business going and was in control of Cleveland Town on Banana Island.

A report in, a trading journal, "The Sierra Leone Watchman" tells the story of how William, who loved to entertain, had planned a big party for the chiefs and traders in the area. He had even invited his estranged cousin Stephen Caulker to the party. Stephen who was not one to turn down a good party, came and had a good time. On his way home from the party, he announced in a very loud voice, to one of Cleveland's men, that he would not step foot on Banana Island again, until he had besieged and conquered it. Just as he had planned, the message reached William. But he thought Stephen must have been drunk when he said it. He had no idea that Stephen had already decided to avenge his brother's death.

Although Stephen did not really want to wage war against the Clevelands as such, he desperately wanted to pay Bemba back for what he had done. He solicited help from the Koya Temne chiefs—King Farama and King Tom who gladly agreed to help him, because they too hated Bemba who had killed or sold many of his people and his own relatives into slavery.*(Fyfe,1964)*

Stephen and his men first went to Bemba's property at Cape Shilling, but having heard about the impending attack, Bemba had fled to Banana Island. Since Bemba was not at Cape Shilling, the attackers took 200 to 300 of his people captive, and killed about 20 of them. Stephen and his men then proceeded to Banana Island, where they found several slave ships waiting for their cargo of slaves. Those who were running away from the attack sought refuge on board the ships, but a horrible thing happened to them. The ships captains packed them in and sailed off with them, leaving behind the slaves for whom they had been waiting. When Cleveland heard about the attack, and finally realized what was happening, he packed up all his people and all the possessions he could carry on board any passing slave ships. On February 3rd 1798, he moved to Sherbro Island *(E. Louise 2001)* and eventually went on to the mainland, where he ruled the lands along the river Jong. *(Kup 1975)*

Stephen seized the Banana Island, and took every thing of value. Everything portable was transported to Plantain Island and the houses were burned down. Those who had been left behind, were taken as prisoners of war. James Cleveland/Corker's grave was trashed and leveled to the ground, so that there would be no memory of him on the island. His headstone was removed and taken to Tasso, the Corker family's burial ground. Stephen ordered his men to place it at the entrance of the cemetery, so that whenever a Corker/Caulker was taken for burial, people would step on the stone when they entered. In essence, this was viewed as a curse against the Cleveland family. (*Kup, 1975*).

To this day, the stone lies at the entrance to Tasso, but it now becomes submerged at high tide. The cemetery is protected by the poro and no non-member or woman can enter without special permission.

William Clevland continued to fight the Corkers and recruited Mende warriors to help him. The Mende warriors succeeded in overrunning the lands of chief Ya Cumba, which were also Corker territory, and constantly raided the area for slaves. The Sherbro chiefs also entered the war and the fighting raged on. This, of course pleased the European slave traders, who supplied arms and reaped a rich harvest of slaves, captured from the devastated villages. In 1803, Governor Dawes who had replaced Governor Clarkson in the Colony, had tried to negotiate a peace but failed in his attempt. In 1805, Governor Ludlam who replaced Dawes, succeeded in brokering a truce with the help of a Mr. John Kizzel, a freed slave who was now a trader and knew the parties well. The Shebro people agreed that, since the British had been given rights to York Island years before, the governor had a right to interfere in the conflict and even to crown their king. (*Kup,1975*)

Meanwhile, the directors of the Freetown Settlement (the new Colony), were looking for a place to settle the freed slaves who had been arriving from different places since the first boat load arrived in 1787. They included, the Nova Scotians from Canada, and the belligerent Maroons from Jamaica. They even considered a proposal to acquire the Banana islands as a home for the Maroons, to avoid putting them in the same area with the Nova Scotians.

Since Chief Stephen Caulker, (*by now the name Corker had permanently changed to Caulker*) was friendly with the colonial authorities, (*In fact, two of his sons, George Stephen and Thomas Stephen, had been taken to school in Clapham, England by the then acting Governor Zachary Macaulay*) he willingly agreed with the proposal. However, during the negotiations there was a debate about who owned Banana Island, since Chief Bai Farama, and the now exiled William Cleveland *(the name Clevland had also changed to Cleveland)* were also claiming to be its owners. Stephen understood the Colony's predicament but was reluctant to give up his family estates which he had just reclaimed. After negotiating for a long time with the Colony Directors, Stephen offered half of the islands for £10,000.00, but knowing the volatile history of the area, the directors were reluctant to accept the offer. In the end, they gave up the idea, because they could not afford to pay the price and did not want to become involved in any disputes with either Bai Farama or William Cleveland. Instead, the Governor tried to persuade Chief Bai Farama to sell a piece of land between Pirate's bay and Whiteman's Bay. But that site was already taken. In the end, they decided to settle the freed slaves on the northern Bullom shore and the Banana Islands were left to the Caulkers. *(Fyfe, 1964)*

Chapter VI

The Influence of Education and Religion

Education has remained the Caulker Family's greatest asset. It has always opened new vistas of opportunity and inspiration to give service, with the consequent improvement in the quality of life of the community in which we live.

Because of our long history of being educated, a Caulker elder, Dr. John Karefa-Smart, admonishes us: *"We the Caulkers must never forget that we have a heritage of enlightened leadership".*

But one cannot discuss the education of the Caulkers without a discussion of the work of the missionaries from the United States.

In his book "Ambassador of Christ and Caesar" Dr. William Fitzjohn, explains:

> *"For over two hundred years, most of the educational activities in Sierra Leone were mainly dependent on Christian missionary organizations of Europe and America. The earliest educational activities in Sierra Leone were undertaken by Portuguese priests at the beginning of the 17th century. Thus it is recognized that from the earliest days of the colony, missions took a most important part in the educational system . . . There is a good deal of truth, as reported by some authorities, that the work of education was begun, and for many years, carried forward almost entirely by missionary efforts, and that had there been no missionaries, there would have been at any rate until modern times, little western education in Sierra Leone.*

The Church Missionary Society (CMS) and the Wesleyan Methodists, began educational activities in the colony in the early part of the 19th century and were followed by the Roman Catholics in 1843". (*Fitzjohn, 1975*)

As early as the 18th Century, among the Africans in the coastal areas, where trading with the European was heaviest from the 1700's-1800's, education was chiefly prized as a means to out-wit European business rivals. Many of the children of the chiefs (including the Caulker children) and African traders, were sent to school in England primarily to learn trading. Some were sent to Liverpool, while others went to Bristol and London. The idea was that since trade was carried out by entrusting large amounts of goods to different people, education would give the children a chance to learn the ways of the whites and 'promote civilization'. Educated children could prevent plundering of their parent's factories and vessels. This is why, families such as the Tuckers, Rogerses, Domingos, Clevelands and Caulkers who were all successful traders, sent their children to school in England. Over the years, like the other families, the Caulkers continued to educate their children in England, but when schools were established in Sierra Leone, they sent their children to those schools.

In London, a special school was established in Clapham by a group called the 'Clapham Sect', which included William Wilberforce, Henry Thornton and others. They were part of the Anti-slave trade organization in England and very much involved in Sierra Leone. The school which was called 'The African Academy', was set up for a specific period of time as an experiment, and was designed to serve as a special non-white project. Many of the African boys received their education at this school, and were taught language, reading and religion. Many converted to Christianity while they were there. One report says that the Clapham Parish register indicates that Stephen John Caulker aged 17 and his brother John aged 12, sons of Stephen Caulker King of Bompeh, were baptized by the Rev. John Venn, Rector, on May 12th 1805. (*Mauser, 2004*)

The boys were never taught mechanical arts, nor were they trained in any occupation which would benefit their country. Before 1808 nearly half of them returned home and took up positions in the Company. Others returned to take on the positions of their fathers as chiefs. They played important roles within their local communities and participated in the coastal commerce. (*Fyfe, 1964*)

The girls were sent to 'Dame schools'. These schools were usually run by school mistresses, who were older women. The girls were taught spinning, sewing, knitting and gardening. When they finished, some of the girls were employed as 'Ladies' maids.' There is the story of a Miss Norie, a relation of the Cleveland's, whose mother was from the Corker family. (She may have been a child of James Cleveland who married a Corker woman.) Miss Norie was educated in England and worked as a lady's maid. When she returned home, according to Fyfe, *she continued to dress in the English fashions, but out of necessity, continued to live like the natives.* (*Fyfe 1964*).

There is also the story of 'Thomas Canrah Caulker', the twelve year old son of Canreba Caulker, King of Bompeh, who, although he was blind, was sent to school in England. He was registered in 1859 in Islington District, Greater London, Middlesex. The story appeared in an English newspaper called the *"Little England's Illustrated Newspaper"*. Here is a part of the story as it appeared in the paper.

"Thomas Canrah Caulker is a son of Canrah Bah Caulker, King of Bompey, etc in the Sherbro Country, West Africa.

He is sent to this country by his royal father to be educated. He will be twelve years old on the 26th of May next. He has the elements of good character, but, as he is only a child, they are not yet fully developed. He is a boy of noble bearing: rather shy, and not at ease with strangers, and you require time to gain his confidence; but when once gained, he is sincerely and thoroughly affectionate. He is peculiarly sensitive of giving pain and when at any time he thinks he has hurt your mind, he is very anxious, by apology and love to make amends. He is naturally not altogether good tempered, but he has been able, in a great degree, to overcome this evil, and now possesses amazing self-command. He is inclined to be very obstinate, but when calmly reasoned with and shown the propriety of doing what he may at first object to do, he will reflect for a time, and invariably do what is thought proper.

THOMAS CANRAH CAULKER, An African Prince,
In the Costume of his Country.

He has excellent common sense, and shows it at times beyond his years. He is exceedingly thoughtful and profits much by reading and conversation, to both of which he pays great attention.

Of his truthfulness, we cannot speak too highly. He has never been known to tell anything like an untruth, or to show an endeavour to deceive in any way: and nothing arouses his indignation more than any attempt to deceive him.

His mind and manners are exceedingly delicate; he is too dignified ever to be rude or vulgar, and an objectionable word was never heard to escape his lips; while he is fond of fun and enters into a witticism or smart remark with great zest, he dislikes rough and vulgar persons, and much admires gentleness and elegance, of which he seems to have an intuitive perception.

For the last two years, he has been unable to see to read or write, but by being read to and questioned, he has a pretty good knowledge of the history of England, of Rome, and something of Greece. He has traced the map of Africa (with his fingers, since he could not see), and knows pretty well the situation of the chief countries in Europe, with a partial knowledge of the inhabitants, productions and climate. With the elements of general knowledge and science he is pretty familiar for his age, and knows a little grammar. He finds a difficulty with figures, but is making progress.

Considering his nerves are by no means strong, he is remarkably patient and even cheerful under his great affliction, and it is only now and then, when a dark cloud comes over him and he feels he cannot do what others can, that his head is ready to burst.

He is happy at school with his companions who sympathize with each other. He bears an excellent character there, and is much beloved by all in the establishment. Since last August he has acquired the art of reading fluently with his fingers in the embossed type any chapter in the New Testament and is learning to play some simple tunes on the pianoforte as well as geography, arithmetic, and writing in the way they teach the blind. His general acquaintance with the Scriptures is good and he is quite familiar with most of the facts recorded in the Old and New Testaments.

After a few years more of instruction and training, if his life be spared to return to his own country, although he is blind, he may be of great use to his countrymen in reading and explaining the scripture to them.

He takes great interest in missions and it is said, is thoroughly alive to Mr. Mofatts's and to Dr. Livingstone's travels and discoveries. He has had read to him all the missionary intelligence up to the beginning of February when he returned to school. This African prince is in the excellent Institution for the Blind at St. John's Wood, and his father pays for his education . . ."(Little England's Illustrated Newspaper

When they returned home, the students were welcomed in the typical African way, with great celebration—Dancing, feasting and entertainment, which lasted from several days to almost a week.

The influence of the Missionaries

After the well documented Amistad affair, the boat load of Africans who had been captured off the Long Island, New York coast of North America, and eventually freed by the United States Supreme Court, were sent home in 1841. The US court had agreed that they had been forced in slavery. Five missionaries of the American Missionary Association accompanied them and established three mission posts, several miles south of the colony. The Good Hope Station, at Bonthe, the Kpa Mendi, on the Jong River and the Mo-Tappan on the Big Boom River. Approximately ten years later in 1855, missionaries of the United Brethren in Christ (UBC) arrived.

When the missionary work of the United Brethren in Christ began, the first missionaries Rev. William Suey, Rev. D.C. Kumlar and Rev. D.K. Flickinger, who arrived on February 26th 1855, were sent to the AMA mission at Bonthe. They stayed at Good Hope and spent several months exploring the country side, looking for a suitable site. After a long visit in Sierra Leone, Rev. Flickinger returned to America without deciding on a place. When he returned in June of the next year, he continued to look around for possible sites, even looking as far away as Liberia. Chief Thomas Stephen Caulker (Ba Tham) of the Shenge/Plantain chiefdom, agreed to give them one hundred acres of land free of charge, on condition that the sons and daughters of the Kagbor country received free education for ninety-nine years. The missionaries began their work in 1857 and provided free education as agreed. But in 1898, after the destruction of the school buildings during the Hut Tax war, school fees of 4 pence a month were introduced.

Although he had given them the land, Chief Thomas Stephen was very in-hospitable toward the missionaries. He actually refused to speak with them, and kept his people from attending church meetings. One can only speculate as to why he was so hostile. Unfortunately the American missionaries seemed to have arrived with the assumption that the people they were going to meet were heathens. Bishop J.S.Mills of the United Brethren Church in his 1898 book "Africa", wrote, *"Thomas Stephen who was where our mission was located at Shaingay, continued a heathen till early 1871."* (Mills.1898.

In an 1855 article in the 'Journal of Sierra Leone African Travels', W. J. Shuey, one of the original UBC missionaries wrote: *"The native African is without a definite system of religion although he knows there is and believes in a God. He believes in witchcraft and necromancy, in the existence of evil spirits and a thousand superstitious follies . . . The heathen of Africa have not the most distant conception of the nature and obligations of the Christian religion and it is not without a long and persevering effort that he can be prevailed upon to renounce his country fashions and idolatrous worship, for a new and untried system of life or practice . . . The negro is adjudged inferior to his fellow man in every respect and is not possessing capabilities of improvement equal to those of the Anglo Saxon race and indeed, some have denied him a rational soul, thus ranking him among the brute creation."* (Shuey, 1855)

Writers Don Carter and Paul Vreugdenhil suggest further reasons for this resentment. *"In general many of the American Missionaries sent to Africa by foreign missionary societies failed to understand the social organization and traditional beliefs of the African people. In numerous cases, they did not even bother to learn the local languages or dialects of the people they were trying to work with. These missionaries tended to assume an attitude of the superiority of Christian beliefs and western culture. Africans were considered benighted heathen, barbarians to be converted to western ways and Americanized. In many ways Africans were assumed to be inferior to westerners in intelligence and culture. Converted Africans were expected to wear western clothes, assume Christian names and adapt to western thinking, manners and customs . . . Because of this lack of empathy for the African, lapses in the progress of the mission often took place."* (Don Carter/Paul Vreugdenhil)—Wikipedia article . . . 1/5/2000.

Another possible reason for the seemingly negative attitude towards the missionaries was the fact that the UBC missionaries disliked all secret societies and disapproved of them. Indeed, they disapproved of the Poro Society, calling it "Devil Worship", even though it was the strongest political force in the country at the time and Thomas Stephen had not long before, established a Poro bush in Shenge.

The missionaries either did not know or they ignored the fact that Thomas Stephen (Ba Tham) had been educated in England and that when he returned home, he had worked as a teacher for the Church Missionary Society, and spent some time translating hymns into the Bullom language. They simply assumed that being African and a member of the Poro Institution, he was a heathen. On the other hand, Thomas Stephen also had first hand knowledge of the Slave Trade and the role white men played in the enslavement of his people. So it must have been difficult for him to trust the message of these white missionaries. Given their attitude, the chief must have deeply resented the fact that the missionaries saw him as a heathen. *(Fyfe, 1962)*

The chiefs in the area also suspected the missionaries of threatening their power and felt that their suspicions were true, when the UBC pastors, and the Creoles, preached at Shenge and Bagru about paying taxes. Although they were polite, and said nothing about their feelings, the chiefs very likely held their grudges and their peace until the time to revolt came. They probably already knew that there would be a revolt.

So it was that after all their work over fifteen years, the United Brethren in Christ could only count two converts, one of whom was Lucy Caulker, the chief's daughter. It is said that when she converted, the chief was so angry, one story claims he sent her away to become the mistress of a European trader. Another story claims he gave her in marriage to a Moslem trader who lived on York Island. *(Fyfe, 1962)* 1962

In 1870, the UBC planned to close their mission. But they decided to make one more try. They sent a Black Missionary and his wife—Joseph and Mary Gomer into the mission field.

Mary and Joseph Gomer

Joseph Gomer was a carpenter who had no theological training and little education. He had taught himself to read and write, but had been a church leader. He and his wife were skilled in practical things. And they established schools, farms and built churches in the chiefdom and generally made a great impression on the people. When they arrived in 1871 he and his wife were able to 'convert' Thomas Stephen just before his death. About this event J.S.Mills wrote this, *"During a meeting held by Rev. Joseph Gomer, the chief was converted and died a Christian on August 28."*1898 (Mills) Africa.

In 1876, Joseph Gomer was ordained when he returned to the United States on leave. He died in Shenge in 1892 where he is buried. *(Darrell Reeck, UM History 10/13/2006) Mary and Joseph Gomer.*

The Missionaries and Education

Since the main goal was to spread Christianity, into the interior of the country, the mission board thought it would be a good idea to train the Africans as teachers and ministers. Rev. Rufus Clark and his wife donated $5,000.00 to build the Rufus Clark and Wife Training School, which became the first secondary school outside the Colony.

The Rufus Clark School as presented in AFRICA by J.S Mills (pp102)

This school was opened on February 21, 1887 with eight students, under principal D.F. Wilberforce, an African who had been educated in Dayton, Ohio. Indeed, the missionaries left their mark on the Caulkers. Many of those who attended the Rufus Clark School at Shenge were the pioneers who took education and Christianity into the interior of Sierra Leone. These pioneers, included men such as, Rev. D.H. Caulker, who went into the Kono country in 1910, Rev. Stephen B. Caulker, Dr. A. T. Sumner, Rev. Alphonso T. Caulker(who later became chief), Rev. Michael M. Caulker, Mr. Benson Caulker, and Mr. Henry Griffith Neal-Caulker. The latter two were among the first teachers at the Bo government school. To this day the Konos respect the Sherbros for their contribution to their enlightenment.

One graduate of the Rufus Clark and wife school, was Joseph Hannibal Caulker, son of Chief George Stephen Caulker II. He was sent to Otterbein College, in Westerville, Ohio to further his education. At the time, Otterbein was a small United Brethren College, which trained missionaries.

An article in one of the college news papers reads, **"African Prince educated at Otterbein."**

When Otterbein's second Black student enrolled in 1896, the college was blessed with royalty—literally. Joseph Hannibal Caulker was not only the second African-American to attend Otterbein, but he was also a prince of Sierra Leone, West Africa.

Caulker arrived at Otterbein in the same year W.E.B. Dubois was attending Harvard University, became the first African-American to earn a PhD in history.

The man considered to be Otterbein's first Black student arrived 37 years before Caulker. William Hannibal Thomas came to "the quiet peaceful village" in Westerville, Ohio, in the winter term of 1859-60, but attended for only a few weeks.

Caulker, who attended Otterbein for five years, had completed the course of instruction at Clark Training school in Shengeh, Africa before coming to Westerville. After completing the Clark curriculum, Caulker remained at the institution for two years as a teacher.

According to Otterbein records, Caulker was called a "conspicuous example of the all-round student." While a student here, Caulker performed in the Glee Club, the Volunteer Band and played three different instruments in his spare time.

Joseph Hannibal Caulker
Otterbein College, Westerville Ohio, U.S.A 1898

The Prince also placed second in the state oratorical contest and captured the school's record in the 100-yard dash with a time of 10.25 seconds.

His memoriam hailed him as a man whose "lips were free from slanderous words and envious speaking. With malice toward none, with charity for all, he was certainly the most popular man in all the University."

This most popular man died in 1900 when he was terribly burned in an accidental explosion. According to college records, the explosion occurred one evening while Caulker was lighting a fire with coal-oil in a dormitory. Caulker, who was within months of receiving his degree, died the next day. The first edition of the Sybil, the Otterbein yearbook was dedicated to his memory.

His memoriam which was included in the first College yearbook, called Caulker's education at Otterbein **"a preparation for his great life-work to which he had set himself, the uplifting of Africa. For her he toiled and labored, for her he prepared himself, to her he would in God's own time return"**

Caulker died before having the opportunity to return to Sierra Leone and fulfill his dream of using his education to uplift his country and the continent of Africa.

He was buried in Otterbein Cemetery. College records do not mention why Caulker's body remained in the United States". (Otterbein Publication)

Although Joseph's time at Otterbein ended tragically, many members of his family followed in his footsteps and graduated. Richard Kelfa-Caulker '35, John Karefa-Smart '40, Amelia Caulker-Ben Davis, '59, Lloyd Bailor '60, Imodale Caulker-Burnett '63, Annie Lefevre-Bangura '67, Princess Caulker-Barlay '67, Phlorence Caulker-Ofili '70, Melvyne Caulker-Yobah '74, Leonard Sumner '90, Mark Hunter '98.

In June 1995, Joseph Hannibal Caulker was awarded a Posthumous Bachelor of Arts degree. The ceremony was attended by his nephew Stephen Bar Thebin Caulker (who received the diploma), Many Caulker descendants were in attendance.

Stephen Bar Thebin Caulker at the grave of Joseph H Caulker, Otterbein College, Westerville, Ohio, USA 1995

The Women's Missionary Association

On October 21 1875, the Women's Missionary Association of the UBC was organized, and immediately began work with the General Mission Board. They soon went to Sierra Leone and set up a mission, at Rotifunk, which is the seat of the Bompeh Chiefdom, about 50 miles from Freetown. They were given a piece of land by Chief Richard Caulker, for their work. Unfortunately, it was the same land which had originally been given to the Lokkos, and their chief Sori Kassebe, as a reward for assisting Chief Richard Caulker in his fight during the Yoni Invasion. The Lokkos were offended by this act, but they held their peace.

The mission work in Rotifunk was begun in 1877 by a woman—Miss Emily Beeken. She was followed by a Mrs. M. Mair. The female missionaries built a chapel, and a school—the Mary Sower's School and Boarding Home for girls, to which Caulker girls were sent. A boys' home, a workshop, a store house and a home for the missionaries were also built. By 1898 they had employed eight Americans—two physicians, five teachers and a mechanic. They also hired eight African pastors and teachers.

Mary Sowers school for girls—Rotifunk—as shown in "AFRICA' by J.S.Mills (p98)

In 1895, Governor Cardew, the governor of the colony at the time, wrote about the Rotifunk missionaries in one of his dispatches.

At Rotifunk it was a pleasure to observe the advance that had been made in the school and industrial training of the native youth through the efforts of the American mission of the United Brethren which was established there for some years. This work is principally carried on by ladies from the United States under the superintendence of a minister, but I fear at great sacrifice of health and life. The system of education is complete and is principally imparted by object lessons. Among other apparatus in use is a human skeleton for instruction in anatomy and physiology, and a combination of spheres to demonstrate the planetary system. The industrial training is practical and consists of brick making, building and carpentry. The bricks however, owing to the great admixture of sand with the clay are of very inferior quality. The establishment of mission stations on such lines as the above cannot but be productive of much good in the interior and the civilizing influences of the one at Rotifunk were very apparent on the natives of the place (Fyfe, p261, 1964)

But on May 1st 1898 the Hut Tax war came to Rotifunk. Because the missionaries had no transportation out of the town either by boat or hammock, they tried to walk but were turned back by the attackers. They were seized and stripped and some of them were raped. In the end, all were hacked to pieces, and their mission was destroyed. The Mary Sowers School for Girls was also destroyed and the seventeen students who were resident, ran away.

The New Secondary Schools

In 1890, Madam Yoko, who was paramount chief of a large area in the Mende country, made an agreement with the Kaiyamba family and gave six acres of land to the UBC mission to establish a new school for girls in Moyamba. The school was built after the war and in August 1900, the first eight boarders moved in. One of the girls was Mabel Caulker, daughter of Chief Thomas Canreba Caulker. She later became the mother of the Karefa-Smarts.

By 1918, for the first time, the students participated in the Government Elementary Certificate Examinations. Meanwhile, back in the United States, in 1921, the Women's Missionary Association, which had first opened their mission in Rotifunk, were celebrating their Golden Jubilee in the United States and decided to name the girls school after its president, Mrs. Lillian R. Harford. Many Caulker women have since been educated at the Harford School for Girls, and three Caulker descendants, Mrs. Elsie Mae Kallon, Rev. William Fitzjohn, Rev. Doris Lenga-Kroma, have been principals of the school.

The late Amelia Ben-Davis (nee Caulker) had this to say about the missionaries of Harford School:

> "In the lives of the first girls enrolled, the missionaries fulfilled the roles of parents, guardians, teachers, spiritual advisors, nurses and friend . . . Those missionary pioneers are living images in the minds of Harfordians, because their footprints laid the solid foundation, which continues to be the bulwark of the strength of character and personality of the average product of Harford School. They and their successors taught and demonstrated the principles of good Christian living, and inspired appreciation for the essential things of life, centered around the knowledge and the fear of God and faith in Him . . .

We learned a lot about the leisure time activities of young people abroad, through music, art and drama, but best of all, we were encouraged to appreciate and to preserve our own culture through our games, folklore and dress. Appreciation of beauty outside of buildings was abundantly expressed and inspired in the careful cultivation of many flowers the names of which we were taught; mock orange here, flamboyant tree there, corralitta, patches of nicely kept green grass with paths bordered with beautiful Easter lilies, and oh, so many others.

It is natural that older Harfordians treasure very highly what they consider their golden heritage, deeply buried in the past and like most human generations, believe that theirs were the best days." (Ben-Davis Article 2000)

1904, the need for a boys' secondary school which would be equivalent to the new girls school in Moyamba arose. The new school was to provide an opportunity for boys from up country to gain advanced education. Originally the mission board had thought of building the school in Shenge, where Rev. Ira D Albert, a missionary, was stationed at the time. But after several meetings it was decided that Shenge could not support such a large school, because access to the town was difficult. It was therefore decided that the school would be built in Freetown. A modest building was rented on East St and on October 4th 1904, the school was commissioned. It was named the Albert Academy, after Ira D. Albert, who had died in a boat accident by the time it was opened. Rev. Raymond P. Dougherty was its first principal and Mr. Edwin Hursh was Vice principal. Five students were enrolled, but by the end of that year, there were six students.

That same year $5,000.00 (five thousand dollars) was donated in memory of Rev. Ira D. Albert by his cousin, for a more permanent building and the Women's Missionary Association donated an additional $5000.00. A piece of land was purchased on Berry Street, on the side of Mount Aureol.

The corner stone was laid on January 1907 and the new building was completed one year later. The first five students were able have their graduation ceremony on the grounds of the new school. Courses at the Academy included general academics, industrial training and intensive religious studies. The goal was to prepare each student for leadership roles in their communities and in the country as teachers, preachers or other interests. Woodwork, metal work and industrial printing were soon added to the curriculum

In Freetown, boys and girls were separated in secondary school, although the schools were paired—The Annie Walsh Memorial school had its C.M.S. Grammar School, The Methodist Girls High school had its Methodist Boys' High school, St. Joseph's Convent had its St. Edward's School and now Harford school had its Albert Academy. The administrators probably hoped as they did for the Grammar School and the Annie Walsh, that the male students at the Albert Academy would be able to choose wives with similar levels of education, from the equivalent girls' schools and would complement them. *(This idea may have worked in the early days, but it hardly works today).*

Post card showing laying of the foundation of the Albert Academy at the Berry Street Campus, January 1907

In Freetown, although a number of Krio students attended the school, the Albert Academy was known as 'the Mende man College', a derogatory term, coined by some residents of the Colony, to demonstrate their resentment at having 'country boys' in their midst. Never-the-less, the school grew, and as happened in the girls' school in Moyamba, many Caulker boys were part of the student body.

From 1939-1959, Richard E. Caulker, (later known as Kelfa-Caulker), an alumnus of the school, served as the first African principal. From 1961-1985, another Caulker descendant—Mr. Max Bailor served as the second African principal. Since then all the principals have been African.

The influence of Christianity and Education in a Caulker home

Evidence of the influence of Christianity and education on the Caulkers, is shown in an article "**Christian Experience in an African Christian Family**" written by Richard Caulker in 1952. This story describes the life of a child in a Caulker home and is included, because every Caulker who grew up in Sierra Leone, whether in the village or in the Colony, as late as the 1960's, can relate to it. This was the way of life in most homes, with few variations.

"Mother always kept a big house. In addition to us youngsters born into the family (seven boys and two girls), there were always some cousins staying with us, as well as four or five other children from relatives and friends who wanted mother to "train" their children.

In the evening, we children played outdoors in the moonlight or by the fire light. We would sit around and tell stories, or play hide and seek and other African games. Between eight and nine o'clock we would be called for the evening prayers, and we all sat on the mat on the floor, except father and mother who sat on the chairs. We would begin by singing from the old Ira D. Sankey Hymns in English which we did not understand, and of which only father and mother usually sang the verses while we joined in the chorus. Sometimes father translated the song into the native language (Sherbro) and after learning the tune, all of us would sing lustily. Father and mother would read the Scripture, verse by verse responsively, after which father would make a short exhortation in Sherbro. We would all go on our knees, and father or mother would pray. Father prayed most of the time in English, but mother always prayed in Sherbro.

In the early days, most of us children slept on mats but, as we grew older, we were put in beds. In the morning, we would be awakened by mother, who then proceeded to see that everyone washed and cleaned up. This was usually between 5:30 and 6:00 o'clock. After that, we did the chores. The girls made beds, swept the rooms and cleaned the house generally. The boys swept the porches, always sprinkling water on the earth floor to keep down the dust. Others swept the yard, gathering up the dead leaves from under the orange and kola trees and, in the process, leaving interesting patterns on the ground with the hard piassava broom. Fires would be started in the kitchen, and a warm bath made ready for father and mother by the older girls. Usually, the boys bathed once a day, in the evenings. The girls had to bathe twice every day, at dawn and night fall and always in cold water. This was part of the "training".

When father and mother were ready between 6:30 and 7:00, mother rang a bell from the living room window. The little bell tinkled around the yard and everybody assembled in the living room for morning prayers.

These were usually conducted in a much more formal atmosphere than the evening prayers. Even other people walking up the road and chattering, would sometimes be cautioned by father or mother from the window, to go quietly as 'anin ha seli' "people are praying". Prayer time was always singing and reading of Scripture and the reciting in unison of certain memorized passages such as the 23rd Psalm. Then we sang a hymn in English or Sherbro. Later, Negro Spirituals were introduced, as well as Revival Choruses. These would be patiently taught by father, sometimes as an evening exercise, and then sung in the morning either just before the prayer or the benediction. After the benediction, mother would tap on the table and all of us would say, "Good morning papa, good morning mama, good morning friends."

The assignment for the day followed prayers and after breakfast, everybody would go "to the work". Father kept a little "porch school" at which he taught us to read and write and sing. Sometimes I think of the pains he took to teach us a song in English when we did not know what a single word meant, and yet he would take a song line by line, verse by verse, and patiently teach it until we had learned all the verses, and could sing them from memory. We would be in "school" for three or four hours a day, depending upon what other business he had on hand: and whenever business took him out of town, we had a holiday, although mother would try to make us "go and study." The rest of the time we spent at play or in doing our little duties. The older boys and girls did heavier work, such as pounding the rice, doing the laundry, getting the fire wood or driving the birds away from the rice farm.

On Sunday, there was no work. As a little boy, even before I knew what the word meant, I learned to say "Sunday is a day of rest." That not only meant no work, but it sometimes meant no play and certainly no noise. In the afternoon we would sometimes be called to study Bible verses, or learn a new song.

Singing—group singing, family singing, singing to "parts"—was always at the core of our family life. Father is somewhat of a musician and reads music very well. In the early days, he had a reed organ at which he played very well. He took sick one time and neglected to shift it around and the white ants got in and "chewed" it up, after which there was never more an organ. But there were always songs and there was always singing. I have never known father to be by himself but he would be humming or whistling a hymn tune as he paced up and down. It seemes he is able to think best when humming a tune. He loves music. Sometimes a prize was given to the one who sang best. Father and mother were always the judges, although they too participated in the contest. But they were always fair and I never knew either of them to win a prize any time. One of us youngsters always won.

Christianity was always an accepted practice in our home. From the earliest times, father and mother kept away for Mohammedanism and pagan practices, and I have never known of a single day at home when we did not meet sometime as a family for prayers. Christian education and worship always held a fascination for father and mother, and from the experience they both had in the Mission School at Shenge (Clark School) they practiced it faithfully. As we children grew older, we were each sent to the Mission school in Shenge and eventually to secondary school in Freetown.

Our life and experience in the church has continued to expand as we grew older. Brother Albert, the eldest son, died while he was serving as head master of Shenge Mission School. After a year of teaching at the Albert Academy, upon my return from study in America, I was appointed Principal of Albert Academy, Solomon, who also studied in America is now a professor in Fourah bay College, Sierra Leone. Bunting the brother next to Solomon, is a private secretary. Glen, who graduated from Achimota College in Ghana, is now teaching at the Bo Government School, Francis has a government scholarship and is at present studying at Guys Hospital in England. Stephen, the baby of the family is now in the government Customs Department in Freetown. Of our two sisters Rachel Coker (Sissy Rachel to us) is with her husband in Freetown, and teaches at the Annie Walsh Memorial School, and Amelia, who for several years was senior teacher at the Harford School at Moyamba, through a government scholarship studied in England and at Otterbein College in America, is now working for the government in the Social Welfare department.

Father and mother live in the old homestead in the village of Mambo. From time to time, we "go home" to see them. It has become a pilgrimage for us children. We visit with them, eat their chickens and oranges and bananas, tell them of our wonderful and varied experiences, then in *the morning and evening we get on our knees with them in the living room and at the family altar." T'is the Blessed Hour of Prayer." The scene has changed little through the years. The house has been rebuilt and made more modern and permanent. There are now enough chairs for everybody: but the songs are still the dear old songs and the heart tunes of yesteryear. As in days gone by, so is it even yet. We rise from that sacred and hallowed family altar with a feeling of having been nearer to God than at any time and anywhere else in the world."* (Richard Caulker) The World Evangel, May 1952 pp 144-146.

The Caulkers are one of the few families who have as many Moslems relatives as there are Christian relatives. This writer's great grandfather, Francis Caulker of Mambo, was himself married to a Moslem woman. It is said he raised his sons as Christians and gave his two girls Sally and Lama, in marriage to Moslem traders. Sally married, Mr. Hadiru Deen and Lama married Mr. Alpha Bundu. On the occasion of their marriage, both girls were given land to develop Moslem communities. The Bundus and Deens have remained close to their Christian Caulker relatives and through these unions, Moslem and Christian live in harmony, and family ties and family values have remained strong in spite of the religious differences.

Part III

Challenges in the family

Chapter VII

The Corkers/Caulkers and the Slave Trade

"The trade of those who were abducted from West Africa and taken to the Caribbean and to the New World by white men, is also known as "The Middle Passage" or the Trans-Atlantic Slave Trade. This event which is considered one of the worst examples of 'Man's inhumanity to Man', occurred while an uncaring and supposedly civilized world carried on with blinkered eyes in a conspiracy of silence and placid acceptance of a system, degrading in its operation and inhuman in its very concept.

But enslaving human beings has been happening since Biblical times. Long before the white man entered the lucrative but debasing African Slave Trade, Arabs, Moors and Berbers had been practicing slavery in Africa, on a massive and monstrous scale, via the Indian ocean to Arabia, to the Middle East and as far east as India, where some Indian Moslem leaders used African Eunuchs as servants in the harems, and the prettiest of the female slaves as concubines for sexual pleasures and gratification. Some Indian rulers often used Africans to build up their private body guards and armies.

Many unfortunate blacks were forced to 'trek' the disastrous 'Desert Passage', which was perhaps much more hazardous than the notorious 'Middle Passage'. Here the Arabs rode on camels while the African slaves, their free movement restricted by metal neck rings and yolks to form coffles, had to walk on the hot desiccating sands of the Sahara Desert, behind long caravans. Many of them perished from thirst, hunger, fatigue and often plain brutality. Those that survived the journey were either taken to the Magreb and across the Straits of Gibralta, to Moorish

Spain, where they served in the ornate palaces of Moorish chiefs and rich merchants. Others were taken via Egypt to the Middle East across the Red Sea, by more conventional methods like Dhows (Arabian Boats), to Arabia and the Middle East. Some went as far as the sultan's palace in Constantinople. This nefarious operation was also widely practiced in East Africa, where Arab Dhows did brisk business ferrying human cargo from the old slave ports of Dar-Es-Salam and the greatest African port of Mombasa, to the Arab lands. Indeed, it could be said that Europeans learned about African Slavery from the Arabs.

It is also forgotten or perhaps overlooked, that many African slaves were taken from the Guinea Coast by the Dutch to South Africa, where they worked on the farms of the Boers. The latter using the hackneyed cliché that 'the Guinea African was more robust and hard working than his Bantu counterpart at the Cape,' which is similar to the claims of the whites in the New World, who averred that the Guinea African was more robust and hard working than Caribs and native Indians of the New World.

When the Dutch East India Company was formed in 1652, Dutch farmers from the Gold Coast came to the Cape of Good Hope, to farm and raise food crops to supply the company's ships on the long voyage to India. They took Africans with them to work their farms. Although these Africans were classified ostensibly as Indentured Labor, they were in fact slaves, who suffered conditions similar to those of their kith and kin in the New World.

In the Americas and the West Indies, the newly arrived Europeans soon began to develop the land which they had appropriated from the original inhabitants, the native Americans or Red Indians, as they were called. At first they tried to use the local Indians as slaves, but it was not profitable, because the Indians could easily escape and go back to their own people. Next they tried shipping large numbers of 'whites' (mainly prisoners and prostitutes) from Europe as indentured servants, but again this did not work very well, because it was easy for the indentured servants to escape and mingle with the free white crowd. In the end, they turned to Africa for slave labor, because their dark skin color and the great distance from their homeland across the Atlantic Ocean, made it difficult for them to escape. Often, the Europeans, many of whom professed Christianity, went to Africa with Bible in hand "to preach the Gospel of

Christ to the natives". They were eager to pass on their beliefs and have the natives conform to them and to their culture. But the missionaries often complained that, "The people ridiculed their attempts to convert them to Christianity." Indeed, there was little to attract the Africans to a religion which was professed by men who it seemed, only came to cheat them when they traded and sell them to those who came in large boats which took them away". **(Francis Caulker) Slavery—The African experience—unpublished Historical novel)**

The African farmers from the coastal area were well known for their rice growing skills, since they had been growing rice for centuries and knew how to cultivate it. Soon the coastal area became known as the "Rice Coast of West Africa", and during the slave trade, plantation owners along the South Carolina and Georgia coasts of North America, were willing to pay a good price for any slaves who came from the rice coast. Subsequently, thousands of people were taken as slaves, from the Rice Coast to North America and to the West Indies. It is estimated that over 14 million Africans were taken by force across the Atlantic Ocean in ships which mostly belonged to the British. In the 1760s, when the trade was at its peak, ships left British ports for the West African coast almost every other day, to trade in human beings. This was probably the worst 'Forced Journey' in the history of mankind. *(St. Clair, 1999)*

The Transatlantic Slave Trade, was a business by which thousands of people made a lot of money, taking millions of African men and women from their homeland, stripping them of their identity, their culture, their humanity, their dignity and their pride.

Like any large business, the Slave Trade involved many people, both in Europe and Africa, thousands of whom probably had no idea what the impact of their work would be on the world. There were the ship-builders and the construction workers, who built the forts where the slaves were kept while the slave traders waited for the African business men to bring them fresh cargo. There were those who manufactured the guns and ammunition, as well as the chains which were used to shackle the slaves. There were many more people who were involved in making the fabrics, the brandy, the rum and other items which were used for trading in Africa. Then there were those who financed the ventures, like the creditors, the insurance companies and those who provided the foreign exchange. The long list also included, institutions such as the British Government and the Church. In one way or another, whether they knew it or not, all these groups had participated in what was considered at the time, to be a 'Global Economy'. An economy which depended on African slave labor. (*St. Clair 1999*)

Slave holding Islands

As the slave trade became popular around the world, it opened the way for the development of several West African Islands and territories. In Sierra Leone a few islands off the coast, were well known for their association with the slave trade. They were easy to defend, either from hostile natives or from other pirates and therefore they were popular with the slavers and pirates. These islands noted for their history in the slave trade, are Bunce Island (sometimes known as Bance island), York Island, and Plantain Island which was the seat of the Shenge/Plantain chiefdom.

Bunce Island, was the site of one of the largest British slave castles on the Rice Coast of West Africa The slave castle was built about 1670 and like other slave castles on the coast, such as Cape Coast castle and Elmina castle, was the site from which several thousand African captives were exported to North America and the Caribbean. This site was active, until it was closed down in 1808.(*Opala, 2004*).

Plantain Islands—This group of slave holding islands are made up of the main island and two smaller islands. The island was a strategic point from the Yawry bay, the Sherbro River, and the Tucker peninsular. The main island is roughly three miles from Shenge. Here, slave traders used buildings called Barracoons, enclosures which were used to hold slaves until they could be shipped out to North America and the Caribbean. For years, relics of these buildings could be seen on the island. They still had the metal rings which were used for securing slaves, stuck to the old laterite walls. One could also find pieces of once large bottles with short narrow necks, called demijohns. These bottles which had once been encased in raffia-like casings and were used to store wine, were now buried in the sand. (*Francis Caulker*) ***Caulkers—Slavery-The African Experience.***—*Unpublished Historical Novel*

After the abolition of slavery around the end of the 1700's the European settlement on Plantain Island was closed for good.(*Tower*) *The Old Kagbor Chiefdom*.

York Island, which was the headquarters of the Royal African Company, had a large European community. Their slaves were either branded with the letters RAC—the initials of the company, or DY, after the Duke of York. The company continued trading in slaves until 1731, when it replaced slave trading with trading in Ivory, timber and gold dust. It was eventually given up by the RAC as unhealthy. (*Fyfe, 1964*)

John Newton

Mention must be made here of John Newton, who composed the popular hymn "Amazing Grace".

As a young man, John Newton worked for John Hawkins a notorious slave trader. Although he was well liked by his boss, as the story goes, Hawkins' wife did not like him and due to her influence he was treated very badly in that household. Because of this abusive treatment, John Newton finally left Hawkins' employ, and joined another slave ship. He eventually became a slave trader and made several trips to and from Sierra Leone carrying slaves across the Atlantic.

Based on his own experiences, Newton describes the relationship between the traders and the Africans thus:

> *"The natives are cheated in the number, weight, measure, or quality of what they purchase in every possible way . . . The natives in their turn, in proportion to their commerce with the Europeans and (I am sorry to add) particularly the English, become jealous, insidious and revengeful . . . with a few exceptions, the English and Africans, reciprocally consider each other a consummate villains, who are always watching for opportunities to do mischief. In short we have, I fear, too deservedly, a very unfavorable character upon the coast. When I have charged a Black with unfairness and dishonesty, he has answered, if able to clear himself, with an air of disdain, 'What! Do you think I am a White man?' . . ."* (*Fyfe, pp74/75 1964*)

On one of his trips back to the island, he had a vision, and was converted. This experience inspired him to write the popular hymn "Amazing Grace". John Newton left the Islands in 1750 and returned to England where he became a prominent priest. He is also known for other hymns like "How sweet the Name of Jesus sounds". He died as a rector of an English church in 1807 (*Tower), Old Kagbor. Unpublished local book.*

Slave Ownership in Sierra Leone

Slave ownership was nothing new in Africa. It was common for tribes to fight amongst themselves over food, animals, land and trade advantage on the many trade routes in the area. The winners took their war captives and used them to build and populate their villages. A slave owner in Sierra Leone was considered wealthy, because wealth meant, more than just accumulating money. It meant being surrounded by people—having a large community made up of family and several people who did the work (slaves). If a chief or a wealthy man, owned a large number of slaves, it meant that he could build large towns, which subsequently included the slaves as inhabitants. So owning slaves was a good investment. (*Fyfe 1964*).

Since the system of slavery and slave ownership in Sierra Leone, seemed to be so different from what history describes, one wonders whether the Africans were aware of the full impact of the sentence they were imposing on their people when they sold them to Europeans. Indeed, several questions arise: Were they aware that their people would be packed like sardines into the belly of a ship and taken to a place farther than they could imagine? Did they for one moment imagine that when their people arrived at their destination, they would be stripped of their names, their culture, their dignity and pride as men and women? Perhaps in their minds, it could not have been worse than selling them to a chief from the north. But did they really care, or were they just doing a trade? Surely it could not be different from how they treated their slaves.

In Sierra Leone, the inland people traveled long distances to bring their slaves to the coast to be sold in exchange for salt. In those days, salt was a very important commodity. It was evaporated from the sea by the coastal people. It is said that a man would sell his wife for salt. They also bartered for dried fish which was plentiful on the coast, as well as for goods which had been brought by the European traders.

Captives who were not deemed useful to the chief's development plan were sold as slaves. It was rare for anyone to be sold without being charged rightly or wrongly for a crime. Prisoners of war were considered to be criminals and many others were accused of witchcraft. *(Fyfe 1964)*

Rules of Ownership

There were rules of ownership which described how slaves were to be treated.

One could argue that the same rules of ownership applied elsewhere, but there was a great difference. The level of 'comfort' and 'dignity', such as it was, which a slave experienced in Africa, was dependent on the attitude of the slave owner.

Slaves were entitled to food, clothing and shelter, and could get land on which to build their homes.

They were to be trained and disciplined.

They were allowed to own property and could get an inheritance.

They could own their own slaves and could work towards their own freedom. *(Fyfe, 1964.)*

Given the rules of ownership, our ancestors must have believed that those they sold would be treated according to the rules of ownership which they knew and understood. John Newton gives us a view of how the ancestors must have felt about selling those they considered to be their own, to a slave trader. He notes:

> "With regard to the natives, to steal a free man or woman and sell them on board a ship would, I think, be a more difficult and dangerous attempt in Sherbro than in London." (Fyfe, p75, 1964)

As the slave trade accelerated the European traders encouraged the winners of war to sell their captives as well as their criminals. The traders paid for the slaves in manufactured goods. Guns were especially manufactured for the West African Market. Imported tobacco was preferred to locally grown tobacco, and rum and brandy, preferred to palm wine. Payments were also made in Iron Bars. Originally, one bar of iron was given in barter. This eventually became the accepted medium of exchange. So many guns would be sold for so many bars, or so many barrels of rum or brandy, for so many bars. 50 bars could buy a slave or a consignment of tobacco instead of the required bars.

The African customers, soon learned to insist on a certain amount of high valued bars. They learned to sell their slaves in lots, so that they could include sickly individuals among those who were healthy in one lot. Sometimes they refused to do business without first being offered a drink. As they grew more experienced in the trade, the price for one slave increased. By 1678, the price had risen to 18-24 bars per slave and by 1725 the price was 40-60 bars. *(Fyfe 1964)*

The Role of the Caulkers in the Slave Trade

The Caulker involvement in the Slave Trade, is one which has caused much embarrassment for some members of the family, especially those who live in the United States. It is a subject which, to the best of this writer's knowledge has never really been discussed within the family.

During this period of the slave trade, as the chiefs, the Caulkers, were the 'land lords and protectors' of their guests. When the traders came with their European goods, their African agents, usually the chiefs' people, bought the goods (probably on credit) which they took into the country for sale. The goal was to return with a supply of slaves which they sold to the trader. Since this was usually a long process, the traders often had to spend their time waiting for customers to take their goods and return with slaves.

French ships also made regular contacts with King Siaka of Genama, head of the Massaquoi family, who supplied them with slaves. There were intermittent wars between the middlemen and the inland vendors. In the Sherbro area, the Caulkers and the Clevelands were still at war. The Mendes from the inland backed the Clevelands against the coastal Bulloms because they benefited from them as slave traders. The slaves resulting from these skirmishes kept up the supply for the trade.

For those who sold the slaves, this trade was more than just maintaining the economy. It was about amassing wealth and power. The Europeans provided guns and other goods in exchange for slaves. The trade assured the landlord (the chief) of continued trade opportunities and revenue, all of which made them rich and powerful in the end. So, as was true in the case of the Corker/Caulkers, after they inherited their mother's chieftaincy, they played a big role in the slave trade, and their wealth and power increased. (Fyfe 1962)

But there were other players in the trade. In the 18th Century (late 1700s), around the time of the abolition of slavery, the trading networks of the Bompeh and Ribbi rivers south of the Freetown peninsular were under the control of the Fula tribe. One of their chiefs, Mori Califa, who had lived in Sherbro for over thirty years, had relatives in the north who supplied him with slaves regularly. It is likely that the other Fula chiefs who were also in the area at the time, did the same thing. The Fulas sometimes took Temne and Sherbro girls as wives, creating half Temne and half Sherbro Moslem children who grew up and joined the melee, waging war. War was good for slave trading.

French slave ships which were unmolested at the time and were safe from the British, also made regular contracts with King Siaka of Genama, the head of the Massaquoi family, who also supplied them with slaves.

The settlers in the Colony began complaining to Governor Turner about being molested and George Stephen Caulker I (Ba Charch) chief of the Shenge/Plantain chiefdom asked the colonial authorities to intervene, as things were getting out of hand. By this time, the Sherbro chiefs were either for or against slavery, and the Caulkers who had originally joined in the trade as employees of the Royal African Company, were now on the side of the colony—against slavery.

In February 1825, Governor Charles Turner came to the area with his own officers and men of the Royal African Colonial Corps. He had a military focus, and was determined to end the slave trade. He also wanted to annex as much of the area as he could. With the help of a naval squadron, he had already reduced the slave trade from the rivers of the north. But he also thought the squadron was ineffective in checking the growing slave exports which continued to flourish in spite of the treaties which had been signed.

He felt that the government was wasting money. So in September 1825, he bought two condemned slave ships and filled them with troops. With no help from the navy this time, he sailed to Plantain Island, where Chief George Stephen I (Ba Charch), was waiting with some of the other Sherbro chiefs. In order to achieve his goal of annexing as much of the region as possible, Turner decided to bargain with them. He told the group that he would do nothing to stop the disturbance, unless they gave up the slave trade and ceded their country to the crown.

On the 24th of September 1825, a treaty in which the Caulkers representing the Ya Cumba House, Banka of Yoni, King of Sherbro and their chiefs, gave up sovereignty and became British subjects was signed. (See The Treaties—Appendix III)

Turner then sailed to Yoni, where the treaty was ratified. The Mende chiefs also promised peace and asked the governor for protection. *(Fyfe 1962)*

Governor Turner, who had been going around the country getting chiefs to cede their countries thus annexing large areas, returned to the Sherbro Island, where he was informed that James Tucker, who had not been part of the treaty signing in September 1825, had refused to give up the slave trade. Reports said that he had gone up the Bum-Kittam river and was preparing to mount a resistance. He had called out the Poro, and had the help of the slave traders in the Gallinas. Turner in turn, mounted an attack, and destroyed the towns along the way. He declared a blockade on the coast all the way to Cape Mount. He lost several of his trusted men during this excursion, including two of his nephews. In the end, governor Turner himself took sick with malaria and died on March 7th 1826. Many years later, William Tucker, chief Thomas Stephen of the Plantain/Shenge chiefdom and Richard Canreba Caulker (who later became a Bompeh chief) and others, came to Freetown and promised to maintain their anti-slave trade agreement.

Christopher Fyfe, puts the slave trade into perspective when he writes,

> *"If the Slave Trade brought wealth and opportunity to the enterprising, the ultimate advantage remained with the Europeans. They used the slaves they bought to create wealth in the transatlantic plantations, while the African vendors received only consumer goods in return, and could not build up capital. If it brought an improved standard of living to the immediate African beneficiaries it nevertheless exploited*

> them, as well as demoralized them, by ensnaring them in an economic system based on callous and inhuman brutality." (Fyfe p 5, 1962)

The End of the Slave Trade in Sierra Leone

The abolition of Slavery came as a blow not just to Europeans and Americans, but to many African slave owners as well. It is clear that our ancestors benefited from having slaves, because they worked on their farms, fished for them and helped to build up their villages and towns. So when the declaration came and the laws were passed, some individuals were resistant to giving up their slaves.

Stephen Bar Thebin Caulker of Mambo House, tells the story of his grandmother's reaction when she heard that she could no longer have slaves.

"Dad had called together all the town's people (who had mostly been family slaves), and told them that they were no longer to think of themselves as slaves. They were now free people. Each family was given a large piece of land on which they could build their own homes and develop their own farms.

My grand mother was a cantankerous aristocratic old lady, but we all loved and respected her. Even the former slaves treated her with great deference. When dad announced that all the slaves were now free, she totally disapproved and did all sorts of little things to show that she did not recognize the former slaves as 'free people. In fact she believed the adage "Once a slave always a slave". Whenever the children from 'downtown' (the area coming up from the river), greeted her with "Good morning grandma" she would snarl back at them angrily and say, "don't call me grandma. I am not grandma to a slave". One day, while dad had gone out on his bike, one of the recently freed families who had built a house on their newly acquired plot of land, were in their back yard. The lady of the house was cooking dinner on thee fire stones. Grandma walked into their compound and deliberately kicked over the cooking pot saying, that they were slaves and had no right to build on her land or cook there. She went on to say that she had paid good money for them and as far as she was concerned they were still slaves.

When dad returned, mother told him what had happened. He immediately went over to grandma's house which was next door to ours. We could clearly hear their raised voices. I had never before heard or seen my dad so angry and as a small boy, I was a little worried about what he would do. He shook his fist at grandma and told her that he was ashamed that she was his mother. (He must have felt strongly about the matter, for him a sherbro man to have been talking to his mother in that way. It was unheard of, even sacrilege for someone to raise their voice to a parent, especially one's mother.) The husband and wife concerned, were so used to being humiliated by grandma, they said nothing. But dad and grandma were yelling at each other and the couple looked confused and terrified as they tried to sweep up the spilled food. By now there was a crowd gathering and grandma who was now shouting more to the crowd than at dad said "you must have been some awful disease that I got rid of when you came out of me!" Dad angrily replied. "Mother, you don't find sour plums under a sweet plum tree. If I am that awful, then I must have inherited it from you." Grandma now burst into tears and placing her hands on her head (a sign of distress used by sherbro women) wailed, "George! you have humiliated me in front of my slaves. Let me lie down now so that you can flog me in front of them, and complete the humiliation!" She was very dramatic about her feelings that day, but as time went on she gradually got over her distress and gave no further cause for complaints". **(Stephen B. Caulker)Article for Caulker Descendants' Association Reunion 2001**

While there will never be any excuses or justification for all that happened, it is important for us as the descendants, to fully understand the times during which the slave trade took place, before we make our judgments. Unfortunately, there is nothing we can do to change the past. But as we learn and understand what happened, we can all work together to make sure it never happens again. Maybe, we can acknowledge that carrying the burden which has been passed down from generation to generation, is wasted energy, which could be put to better use in the struggle to improve our relationships as human beings moving forward in our quest for progress, for ourselves, our country and the world. If we focus only on the negative aspects of our story, we lose sight of the positive influences and wonderful parts of the heritage we have received from our ancestors.

Chapter VIII

The Caulker Wars

1. The Caulker wars, have been chronicled in 'The Caulker Manuscripts, by George Maximillian Domingo, who gives his opinion about the reasons and the execution of the wars. (See Appendix II)

As the story goes, a rumor which said that chief Thomas Kon Tham had a son called Canreba, by a slave woman and that the child was being raised by his mother's people in a town called Gbambayah was circulating in the chiefdom. Thomas Stephen of Shenge/Plantain heard this rumor about his new cousin Canreba, and went to meet him, while he was on a business trip for his brother George. When he saw the child, Thomas Stephen must have recognized a family resemblance and apparently could not deny that the child was a Caulker. So he decided to take him to be with his father. When he was returning to Plantain Island he made arrangements to travel back with the child. The child was then sent from Plantain to Bompeh, where he was warmly welcomed by his new family.

As Canreba grew up, he showed a lot of interest in chiefdom affairs and seemed to have a lot of influence in the chiefdom. Gradually, he became viewed as the power behind the throne—the Crown Prince. After Thomas Kon Tham died, Canreba's uncle Charles was crowned chief, but was considered a 'nominal' chief although as chief, Charles Caulker of Bompeh (also known as Ba Charlay), had opened up the country to the timber trade, which turned out to be very successful. Now both Caulker branches, the Bompeh Caulkers and the Plantain/Shenge

Caulkers, wanted possession of the timber-producing mainland. This of course created yet another reason for war within the family. This time the war would be between Chief Charles Caulker (Ba Charlay), Canreba and their cousin Thomas Stephen, who was then Regent of Plantain and Shenge.

To make matters worse, now that Canreba was becoming more influential, the Plantain/Shenge Caulkers were beginning to question his rights to succession (should the need arise), after all he was the son of a slave woman. Canreba heard this and saw it as a slur on his parentage. This to him warranted revenge. These questions about his rights to succession were definitely another reason for war. So Canreba urged his uncle to re-take the Plantain/Shenge chiefdom, and reunite the chiefdom. The chief agreed with him, and together they began making preparations to attack.

When Thomas Stephen heard about their plan, he began to make preparations to defend his chiefdom. As far as he was concerned, he had a right to the Plantain/Shenge chiefdom, since George Stephen I, the late chief was his brother, and as was customary in Bompeh, succession was from brother to brother, not father to son, as George had clearly intended. Thomas Stephen also felt that he had worked with his brother during his reign and was therefore well qualified to be the Chief. Besides that, it was he who had found the boy Canreba and brought him to Bompeh. So, as far as he was concerned, being the elder cousin he deserved gratitude and respect from Canreba.

Eventually, the preparations were made for this great war, and both parties were ready. But when the time came nothing happened, because there had been no peace talks between the parties. In those days it was the custom, that if there was a dispute between two chiefs, the disputing parties would be called together to settle their differences.

A female section chief named Thetha Yangkei of Ribbi, (*which was then under Bompeh rule*) suggested that a meeting be held for peace talks between the two parties. The Caulker Chiefs agreed to meet in Ribbi to discuss their differences.

But the men of Bompeh and Ribbi, had other plans. They knew that the Caulkers of Bompeh, like the men of Ribbi, were all members of the Poro Society, and the Caulkers of Shenge and Plantain were non-members. Chief Charles Caulker (Ba Charley) of Bompeh and a male section chief of Ribbi, met secretly and made plans to go ahead with their war pretending it was an order from the Poro Society. The irony of this whole thing was, the Poro Society had always been considered a society of peace.

Thomas Stephen arrived in state for the meeting. He travelled in his royal boat with his entourage. They left early that morning and arrived later that afternoon. They anchored and waited for the other boats which were bringing the section chiefs. Among those expected for the meeting were, Ya Cumba of Tasso, Yorgbor of Bendu, Yah Bome of Thumbah, Sopolee of Konnoloh, Sosanthe of Cargbor River and the Chief's nephew Thomas Kugba, (for whom Thomas Stephen was acting as Regent). Thomas Stephen had sent him and another cousin named Charles to school in Freetown, and they returned from school just before the war started.

All the guests were cordially welcomed and given quarters in the southern part of town, in an area where the hosts, (knowing their plan), felt no one could escape. Thomas Stephen did the customary 'Konani' ceremony—presenting 'gifts' for his hosts.

As is customary during events such as this, there was dancing and feasting for three days, before the actual meeting began, and crowds arrived from all parts of the chiefdom. Meanwhile, the Poro men in the chiefdom arrived with concealed weapons—hatchets, swords and guns, which were hidden away, awaiting the order to strike. The plan was to kill the Chief and his entourage, then send troops to destroy Shenge and Plantain. When that was accomplished, the Chief Ba Charlay and Canreba would then establish themselves as chiefs of the entire area.

Fortunately for Thomas, there was a Poro man in Ribbi named Bureh Warkee, whose daughter Ya Concheh, had been one of the wives of the late George Stephen I. *(A majority of the Caulker chiefs, though some were Christian, took multiple wives whom they married by Customary Law,)* As a Poro man, Bureh Warkee had been privy to the secret and knew that the penalty for revealing a Poro secret was death. But he chose to sacrifice his life for his son-in-law's brother. Bureh Warkee went and revealed the plot to Thomas Stephen, who immediately called his staff and gave them orders to prepare to leave immediately. The young men and women in the entourage were to be put into small boats, and taken to the royal boat. The chief then disguised himself and walked through the mangrove swamp in order to get to his boat.

It was not long before the alarm went out that the chief had escaped. The poro members knew that Bureh Warkee, had been the late George Caulker's father-in-law and he was immediately accused of revealing the plot. For his offense, he was executed, and the war boys were immediately dispatched to Plantain Island. When they arrived they found that the Chief was not there.

As soon as Thomas Stephen arrived home, he ordered all the children to be moved to the Daymah islands, (now called The Turtle Islands) in care of Lucia San Bokrah. Among this set of children were, Sophia Caulker (who later became chief Madam Sophia Neale Caulker), Neker Caulker, Lucia Caulker of Debia, and Susannah Caulker, the chief's daughter. When they had left, the Chief went to Bendu and told his friends, Chief Bah Ville of Yainkain, and Chief Lango Blah of Bendu about the incident. While he was at Bendu, he heard the gun shots, and knew that Plantain Island had been attacked and taken.

Although the town on the island had been walled and well fortified, the enemy met with little resistance, because Thomas Stephen had taken his best warriors with him. It was a cold and foggy Harmattan night when the war boys arrived from Bompeh and Ribbi and this had given them the advantage of arriving undetected. The town was easily surrounded, stormed and taken. Only one person was killed. The Caulker women and men who had been left behind were taken prisoner, because Charles and Canreba had given orders not to harm the women or treat them roughly (they were to be tied up with handkerchiefs instead of ropes). The Caulker men who put up no resistance were to be brought to them unharmed. Anyone else not of the family, was to be killed. After the attack, Thomas Stephen returned to Plantain Island, but found the place in ashes. So he gathered the survivors and returned to Bendu.

Mean while Charles and Canreba went with their armies to other sections in the chiefdom, and forced the people to join them in their war. Thomas George Kugba son of George Stephen I, who was angry with his uncle for refusing to give up the chieftaincy when he came of age, joined forces with Canreba. He then left Mambo where he had been living, and built a town which he named Sinclar (now known to marinas as Buoy Point) in the Sherbro River, and made it his garrison. He changed his name to Masso, (a name used by the Bundu Society referring to the fact that traditionally, the new initiates of this female society, are brought out early in the morning by the leader—Masso.) As Masso, Thomas Kugba would always 'move' early in the morning.

Chief Thomas Stephen's son George Stephen II, had been away at school in England for seven years. On his way home, he stopped in French Guinea to gain experience, in preparation for the day he would be chief. At the time the belief was, *"If we mean to be rulers of our people, we should not spend time in idleness. But after gaining all the book knowledge that is possible, we should go to another country and prepare for such an office." Manuscripts (part I pp8)*

While he was in French Guinea, George heard about the war against his father and the destruction of Plantain Island. Unfortunately, he could not communicate with his father, since the route was blocked because of the war and there were no steamers leaving French Guinea for Sierra Leone.

As the war intensified, some volunteers managed to get to George and tell him what was going on. Meanwhile, Thomas Stephen, who was now living as a guest in Bendu, was trying to recruit war boys to help him drive the enemy out of his chiefdom. But he was having little success. Eventually though, help came from two sources—Kiskammah, chief of Mongray and Sehy Keah Bokah, chief of Bagroo both agreed to help but the chief of York Island remained neutral.

In 1842, Chief Charles Caulker died, and Canreba became the new chief. Now, Canreba and Thomas George Kugba (Masso), were successfully recruiting war boys from those parts of the country where the people had been coerced to join them. They kept their newly recruited war boys at Bonthe and Bachuland, as their plan was to go across to Bendu and invade it, hopefully without a struggle.

Both sides took a year to prepare for war. Thomas Stephen built stockades at Bendu Stockades which were built and manned by warriors, and a few war boys. He then moved his people from the surrounding villages into Bendu town. Canreba and Masso daringly built four stockades around those which Thomas had built, but they met with no resistance, since Thomas Stephen did not have enough war boys. War boys generally did not carry stores. They depended on the loot they obtained by plundering. Canreba's war boys therefore plundered the deserted villages, and took whatever they could find.

Thomas Stephen's volunteers who had gone to French Guinea, returned with word that help was on the way. George had arranged for a schooner full of war boys lead by a daring warrior named Jonga or Thomas Nightingale. The warriors arrived, bringing with them much needed gun powder, guns, swords and provisions, just as Canreba and Masso were preparing to attack Bendu. In addition, Sehy Keah Boka the chief of Bagroo also sent a number of his old and experienced war boys. These reinforcements strengthened the Thomas Stephen's forces and he was finally ready for war. But at the time he had a blind boil under his arm which was causing pain, but that did not stop his preparation for the attack

Masso was at his garrison on Buoy Point when Canreba's war boys at Bonthe, sent him a message informing him that they were now near Bendu, were ready to attack. They were confident they could win and were waiting for him to arrive. When he received the message Masso sent an impudent message to his uncle Thomas Stephen, telling him that he was to save the left-overs from his dinner because he would be arriving the next morning.

Morning dawned, but to everyone's surprise, Bendu had not been attacked!! At least not yet. But, led by Charles (Masso's cousin) their leader, the war boys from Bonthe had boarded one hundred and fifty canoes and were crossing towards Bendu. They were indeed on their way. When Thomas Stephen's men saw the boats approaching, they prepared for battle. Before they left, Thomas Stephen spoke to them saying, *"Go! I have done nothing wrong. It is an unrighteous war against me and God will deliver them into your hands."* (Manuscripts Part I, P41)

The head warrior Jonga (A.K.A Thomas Nightingale), was in a Kroo canoe with twelve rowers who sat back to back, so they could go either backwards or forwards without having to move. He also had a bugler, William Domingo, on board. Jonga was determined to win, and swore that if one of the enemy was able to cross over and take Bendu, he would give up his country—Rio Pongas, to Thomas Stephen. On that note, Jonga and his men went out to sea to meet the contingent coming from Bonthe.

When the two sides met, there was an intense fight. The boys from Bonthe attacked first, but Thomas Stephen's boys, headed by Jonga, fought hard, and killed many of them. Infact, most of them were killed. Some were drowned, others shot, and there were many bodies in the sea. It was a gruesome sight! But Canreba and Masso had been defeated !

Meanwhile, those of Canreba's boys who were on land could not enter the Bendu stockades. Their commander, Kehkehbookeh, an experienced warrior, had also been killed, so they retreated. As the war boys fled, they were chased and slaughtered.

Even a Moslem priest who had been seen coming from one of Canreba's stockades with his prayer beads, was shot.

When Masso realized that they had lost, he sought refuge at York Island. His head warrior and cousin Charles was captured, and brought before his uncle, Chief Thomas Stephen. Because he was part of the family, the now victorious Chief granted him pardon and Charles was set free. Two of Thomas Stephen's maternal uncles however, were not so lucky. They were captured and brought before the Chief. When he asked them why they had joined forces with Canreba and Masso they explained that they had been forced to do so. The Chief ordered them killed anyway, in order to prevent them from spreading seeds of discord within his family.

Another captive who was brought before the chief, was a singer from Sacheeh. The chief asked him to sing for him and was so pleased with his performance, he invited him back. The man returned a few weeks later with some of the elders from his village, and asked for protection. He reported that he and his people had been forced to flee, because the chief's war boys were still plundering many of the surrounding villages in which Canreba's boys were hiding. They had also ransacked every corner of Bonthe. To show their loyalty they brought a new wife as a gift for the chief. When the chief accepted his new wife, the singer knew that he and his people would be safe.

Masso, who had been hiding on York Island, eventually left there and came to the Thaimdale district. He had heard that his uncle Thomas

Stephen was still determined to punish those who had waged war against him. Besides, the Chief had sent his troops, headed by his warrior Jonga, to Tasso, Shenge, Bainjaka and Mambo, where they continued to plunder and take captives. They took captives from Bagroo to the Kagboro river, and from Mambo to the head of the Kagboro river. Some of the troops had even gone into Thaimdale where Masso himself was hiding. When he heard that, he fled to Kittam, where he stayed in exile. During this time of self exile, his son William was born. Meanwhile, his cousin Charles, had returned home to Bompeh where he married, and also had a son whom he named Charles Marhew Caulker.

While Masso was in exile in Kittam, he sent a delegation to his uncle Chief Thomas Stephen at Bendu asking him for forgiveness. Thomas Stephen was not really willing to forgive "this ungrateful and treacherous nephew of his", but one of his daughters (possibly Lucy), pleaded for him and the chief relented. When Masso heard that he had been forgiven, he could not believe it and still feared a reprisal. Instead of going to the chief's compound alone, he decided to go with Chief Mannah of Gallinas who was on his way to visit the Chief. With the chief of Gallinas as witness, Masso (Thomas George Kugba) was pardoned.

Following his pardon, Masso returned to Thaimdale where he established himself as section chief and exerted a lot of influence over the people in the area. But Thomas Stephen's war boys continued to plunder and intimidate the people. One of Masso's warriors suggested to the community, that since he, Masso, was back in his uncle's good graces, they could try gaining favor with him so that he would plead with his uncle to at least stop the plundering. The warrior, Kong Dumahbey, advised the community that if they wanted Masso's cooperation they were to bring him a wife—'a young lady of excellent beauty'. So the people of Thaimdale brought Masso a wife. In return for this gift, Masso used his influence with his uncle to stop the plundering in the Thaimdale area. Soon Masso's new wife bore him a son whom he called Francis Theophilus Caulker (later of Mambo).

Masso eventually had to leave Thaimdale because of ill health. He went to Mambo leaving his warrior Kong Dumahbey, in charge. Given this opportunity as the leader, Dumahbey quickly made himself Section Chief of the Thaimdale area.

Masso recovered from his illness shortly after he returned to Mambo. He lived until 1868 and when he died he was buried at Tasso by his son Francis.

As time went on, Thomas Stephen became stronger. Over the years, he had continued to collect war boys, sending them to neighboring 'countries' to subdue them. Eventually he amassed quite an army, and was now ready to pay Canreba back for what he and the Bompeh people had done to him. Canreba was also preparing to defend Bompeh. Rumors of another war began to circulate and the timber trade was becoming affected. (Timber was now being exported to England in great quantities from the Bompeh and Shenge districts). The people in the district were also concerned about the threat of another war. So the colonial traders sent a representative, a Mr. Lemon to the governor, Colonel George Macdonald, who wrote to Thomas Stephen and Canreba, asking them to meet with him for peace talks. Both agreed to meet with him, but Thomas refused to go to Bompeh and Canreba refused to go to Bendu. The governor, seeing that he did not have choice, agreed to meet them at Tasso where they met and agreed to peace. The peace treaty of 1845—Treaty Number 39 was signed in Freetown. (*See Appendix*)

After the signing, Canreba returned to Bompeh and Thomas was to return to Bendu, but for some reason he was detained in Freetown. He stayed there for six months, before he was able to leave with his people who had been refugees in Freetown. On his way home, Thomas stopped at Tasso to pay homage to his ancestors. He promised the ancestors that he would not return to Bendu or make aggressive war again. He then joined his people and returned home to Shenge. Those who returned with him were, Beah Will, Thetha Yang Kate the chief's sister, Thetha Yang Maligah and Thetha Yang Sally, mother of his son Willie S.G.Caulker (*different from William Caulker son of Thomas George Kugba Caulker*), who became Shenge's first cabinet maker.

Now that an agreement had been signed, both chiefs remained peaceful, in their respective chiefdoms. But in spite of their efforts at maintaining peace, there remained great animosity between their children and among their subjects, creating several minor disputes.

Thomas Stephen continued to increase in strength and was highly honored and respected by the other chiefs, who saw him as their superior. Canreba Caulker also became honored a by his surrounding chiefs. He too continued to collect war boys.

There is a local story told about Canreba, which may explain why he was also thought to have supernatural powers. One day, a timber trading ship arrived and after loading it with timber, Canreba boarded the ship. When he did so, the ship listed badly to one side, and the captain called out to him—"Hallo Caulker, do you want to sink my ship?" He was indeed considered to be the mightiest ruler the Bompeh chiefdom had ever produced. He had many children all of whom he had educated. Two of his sons, Richard Canreba and Thomas Canreba later became chiefs.

Canreba reigned for twenty five years and died in 1857. He was succeeded by his brother Theophilus Caulker (locally known as Tham Bum), who had been educated at the Thomas Stephen school on Plantain Island. Theophilus was the father of James Canreba Caulker, who became chief in 1899 and John Canreba who became chief in 1902. When Theopilous died in 1864, he was succeeded by his nephew Richard Canreba Caulker who continued his father's quarrel with the Shenge Caulkers. And so the grudges continued.

The Caulkers finally agreed to make peace in 1870 and signed yet another agreement, Treaty Number 71, on June 11th (See Treaties, Annex III) The locals called the war between the Bompeh Caulkers and the Shenge Caulkers, "Pemm Sabbah"

Thomas Stephen Caulker outlived his nephew Canreba by fourteen years and died in 1871.

* * *

2. The War between William Thomas George Caulker of Mambo, (nicknamed 'the troublesome Caulker) and his cousin Chief Thomas Neale Caulker of Shenge

After Thomas Stephen died in 1871, he was succeeded by his son George Stephen II. At the time, William Thomas George Caulker, grandson of George Stephen Caulker I, and son of Thomas Kugba Caulker (Masso) was absent. After leaving the CMS Grammar School in the 1850s he had gone to trade in the Mende and Gallinas country, and did not return to

Shenge until 1876. By that time, George Stephen II, whom William did not like, had been crowned chief. Angry that he had been overlooked for the chieftaincy, William, his brother Francis, and their families left Shenge and moved back to Mambo which had been their father's home.

As the story goes, one day in 1878, William was invited to Shenge by the well respected United Brethren in Christ missionary Rev. Joseph Gomer. It seemed, Gomer was trying to make peace between William and George Stephen II. But when William arrived, the Chief's men were waiting for him on the beach. He was immediately arrested and taken to the Chief. William was extremely angry. He believed that Rev. Gomer had betrayed him. The Chief would have had William killed if not for Governor, Samuel Rowe, who feared that if William was killed, there would be a war of revenge. So he sent officers to bring William to Freetown, where he was jailed. That same year, Rowe's tenure as governor came to an end, and he was replaced by Governor Arthur Havelock. The new governor was informed that the prisoners, including William, had been jailed illegally. Rather than leave William in jail indefinitely, Havelock decided to continue trying to make peace between the Chief and his cousin. He called George Stephen II to Freetown, but unfortunately, when George Stephen II arrived, he was ill and had to have emergency surgery. He died during the procedure, and was taken to Tasso for burial.

After the death of George Stephen II, Governor Havelock decided that since the Caulker territories had been brought under British rule with the revival of the Turner Treaty in 1861, he could now use his own initiative to crown a new chief. He decided to make George's half brother, Thomas Neale Caulker, who had accompanied George to Freetown, the Regent Chief. His decision completely ignored the traditional process for crowning a chief, and when the news reached Shenge, that they had a new chief, there was great disturbance. Many people, including William of Mambo, were unhappy about the turn of events. But the police had been warned not to interfere. So, Thomas Neale-Caulker became the ruling chief. Although William and Thomas Neale were, on the surface reconciled, privately they remained bitter enemies. **(See Appendix III for Memo. of William Caulker's release.)**

William returned to Mambo where he established himself as a business man. He travelled around for trade and made friends whereever he went. For the three years, following his return, however, people noticed that each time he traveled, he took two or three boys or girls with him, and often returned with only one child. Whenever anyone asked about the children they had seen him with, he would say, "I left them with my wives." No one dared to question him further. Some visitors from the Susu country in the north came to visit one day, and when they were ready to leave, William gave them ten boys and girls to take with them as gifts. The children's parents were so upset they reported the matter to the chief, telling him that they believed William Caulker was sending their children to the north to be sold as slaves, although William had told them that the children were going to work for him. The parents said they would not have minded if their children were indeed working for William, because they would have at least been able to see them occasionally. The chief informed them that because they had turned the children over to William without his knowledge, there was nothing he could do about the matter. But when he realized that the parents were really anxious about their children, Thomas Neale wrote to his cousin Richard Canreba who was the chief in Bompeh, and informed him of the situation. He also advised Richard not to allow the Susu traders through his chiefdom. He then sent a message to William, ordering him to come to Shenge. The messengers returned and informed the chief that William had gone to Tasso to pay homage to his ancestors. Thomas Neale decided he would board his boat and wait for William at the mouth of the Kagboro river.

William had indeed been to Tasso. But that night on his way back to Mambo, the chief had him arrested and brought to Shenge for questioning. William admitted to the charge of taking the children as merchandise and agreed to sign an affidavit, on condition, that his men be released. After he signed the papers he was detained, but escaped a few days later. No one knew how he did it or where he went. They searched all over, but were unable to find him. Thomas Neale reported the matter to the colonial government and with their help the children were found and released.

After the furor died down, William returned to Mambo and set up a small business, with the help of a good friend of his, a Mr. S. Macfoy, whom he had met on his travels, and who now supplied him with goods.

He made a comfortable living and life was good for his family and the families who lived in the town. He was the head of Mambo, and as such, the landlord to all who wanted to live there. But things changed when in 1883, William gave the town of Maneah to a Muslim friend of his to take care of. The man was an Arabic teacher, and had a young student in his care. One day, the boy wandered off and mistakenly entered the Poro bush whilst the society was in session. The members caught the boy and initiated him with no one's consent. When the man heard this, he took his cutlass, and went into the Poro bush, where he was caught and detained. William Caulker was himself a Poro member. So when he heard about this, he went to the Poro members and demanded the return of the man and his boy. The Poro men said that they would have to be paid, because the stranger had violated the Poro law by going into the bush. Since the boy had already been initiated, he would have to stay in the bush until the session was over. William would not hear of this. He told them that as the landlord, he should have been notified about the infraction of the law, by his guest, before they took action. According to the law, he said, if an individual's guest violated any of the laws of the land, it was the duty of those who had been offended to report it to the landlord, before action could be taken. Since they had not notified him, he would pay nothing. The case then went to Chief Thomas Neale, but he was not a Poro man and did not know how to resolve the matter. He advised William to give in, but he refused. So, Thomas Neale referred it to the Colonial Government, accusing William of aiding and abetting a robbery. Once again, William was arrested and taken to Freetown for trial. His friend Mr. Macfoy, got him a lawyer—a Mr. Samuel Lewis, Esq, who won the case but warned William to be careful next time. William returned to Mambo, and his friend and the boy were returned to him.

Meanwhile, Thomas Neale-Caulker was becoming more and more oppressive and harsh, and no one liked him. In fact, he was hated by so many of his section chiefs, that William knew that whenever he needed to, it would be easy to incite them to take action against the chief. All he had to do was wait for the opportunity.

He continued to trade for his friend Mr. Macfoy. But one day, the boat he was in, was attacked and he and his crew narrowly escaped death. Mr. Macfoy blamed William for his losses and William agreed to pay him back over a two year period. Although William worked very hard to pay back the debt, he could not. This destroyed their friendship, although Macfoy did not press him for payment.

One day, while William was away from home, two of the boys whom he had tried to sell to the Susu people in the past, raped two of his wives. When he heard about it, he swore he would deal with them. When the parents heard that William was out to get their sons, they fled with the boys to a neighboring chief, Mudli Sesil, for protection. Mudli was afraid to confront William, so he took some money—£3.00, and went to Chief Thomas Neale. The chief sent for William, but his brother Franklyn warned William of Mudli's visit and told him not to trust the man. Fearing that trouble was brewing, William took all his wives and hid them in a village called Tangnemah. He then went to his cousin Richard Canreba in Bompeh, and reported the matter. In their conversation, he told Richard, that he was going to Petifu and Moyamba to look for help. Richard advised him not to take any action against the boys just yet. He suggested that he wait until he (Richard) had contacted Thomas Neale, to see how this could be resolved. But William paid no attention. The next morning, while breakfast was being prepared for him in the chief's compound, William left and went into the Mende country.

There, William first met with a man named Ndambah who talked a lot about his own dislike for the Shenge chief. The chief had done something for which Ndambah wanted revenge. William agreed to help him, because he felt the man would be able to influence his people. Together, they set out looking for war boys. They collected so many war boys from the Mende chiefs, that they were forced to leave some of them behind. Ndambah promised that he would return for them if they were needed. William continued on his travels through Bompeh district without any problems, until they reached Shenge district and entered Mudli Sesil's town of Larwahnah where the 'rapists' were hiding.

Larwahnah was one of the richest towns in the Shenge District, but on May 24th 1887, (the year the Creoles were celebrating the Centenary of the colony,) William and his boys plundered it. He captured the two boys who had raped his wives, put them in chains and killed them. He then marched his war-boys back to Mambo. When news of the Larwahnah attack got around, everyone in the whole area was concerned and went on alert. They had heard that the war boys were now sweeping through the area, killing people and devastating villages with the ferocity of the earlier wars. They sought refuge where ever they could find it, going into the colony, into to towns and villages like Daymah, Thaimdale, Bonthe and several other places.

News that William had successfully avenged his wives had also spread, and now everyone saw him as the solver of their problems. People came to him, trying to get him to help them settle their differences with the chief. On May 27th Canray Femah, the section chief at Mothenkil, came and told William that he had not liked a decision the Shenge chief had taken in a case which involved him. He was asking William to help him take revenge against the chief. William wisely told him that he was done with fighting. He had done what he had set out to do—avenge the rape of his wives, and would do nothing else. Femah accepted this decision, but warned William that the Komah people would probably try to seek revenge against him, because some of those whom his war boys had killed, were their relatives. Willam said he would bear it in mind, but told Femah that at the moment he was not worried. Soon after Femah's visit, the sons of a resident of Bompeh District came and asked if William could join them in a fight against Chief Thomas Neale Caulker, because they also did not like a decision the chief, had made in the case between themselves and a Mr. J. V. King of Tombo. This time, William agreed to help. He decided it was time to confront his cousin Thomas Neale once and for all. So he sent for the rest of the war boys whom he had left behind in Mende country earlier.

His cousin Thomas Kugba II, (probably a son of the late Thomas Stephen), came to visit him one day, and asked why William was preparing for war. He told him that it was something he had to settle for himself. He also explained that he, (William) was angry with himself. Here he was, older than Thomas Neale, and of superior birth, but instead of defending his rights of succession, he had allowed the son of a bondswoman to rule. He sorely regretted this. Thomas Kugba was sympathetic and offered to help him recruit war boys.

Kugba went home to his village of Sankone, and prepared to travel around to various towns to do the recruitment. He succeeded in getting some money, but most people told him that they were not from Shenge

District, and did not want to get involved. They were choosing to remain neutral. He even went to see a Mr. J.H.Pratt, who was working as an agent of Mr. Macfoy, William's former friend. Mr. Pratt also refused to help.

The only person who agreed to donate some goods to the cause, was a man named Moses Lefevre, who lived in a small village called Bompetoke, near the town of Thombay. Lefevre gave him some supplies. But the people of the village were scared and by the time Kugba arrived they had left to seek refuge, Finally, Thomas Kugba succeeded in getting war boys from the Temne coutry. The boys were happy to get in the job because they knew that they would at least get a lot of loot in a very short time just by plundering.

Meanwhile, Ndambah was on his way back from the Mende country with the reserve war boys to join William in Mambo. Unfortunately for Ndambah, on their way to Mambo the war boys raided a Temne village. This made the people so angry they promised to revenge. When William heard about the raid, he immediately had Ndambah arrested and sent to Freetown. One of his men, Mahmodu Karimo, had to take a large bull as a peace offering to the Temnes.

One of the UBC Missionaries Rev. D.F.Wilberforce, a native of the Imperreh District, had recently moved to Shenge as the headmaster of the Rufus Clark Training School. When he heard about the preparations for war he made arrangements to get some warriors from his home to help defend the school. The Police Inspector, General Captain Halkett, who was stationed in Bonthe, Sherbro Island, also arrived in Shenge, when he heard of the war threats. He brought policemen with him, and placed them in pairs, in the large towns on the border of the Tucker River. A naval cruise ship was also anchored off the Shenge shore. Shenge was now set for the war.

Kong Dumabey (Masso's old warrior) who was now Chief of Mando, was worried about all this war preparation. So he sent three men, Francis Caulker (William's brother), Beah Lehbee and Gbannah Yorma, as ambassadors to William and to the chief, to ask why they were preparing for war. He also asked if they would be willing to meet with him for peace talks. On their way to Mambo, the ambassadors first passed through Shenge and spoke with the chief. Chief Thomas Neale-Caulker sent back to say that, he had done nothing to wrong his cousin. In fact, when he became Regent Chief, and his cousin was in trouble, he had done all in his power to seek his release. He declared that if he had offended William in any way he was willing to reconcile with him. With this message from Thomas Neale, the ambassadors proceeded to Mambo to ask William the same questions. William sent a message back to Kong Dumabey telling him not to interfere, because he (William), was determined to end this contention between himself and Thomas Neale once and for all.

On their way back, instead of going to the Chief, the ambassadors stopped at the village of Bompetoke, where Beah Lebee's cousin John Williams lived. Beah Lebee, told his cousin what was happening at Mambo and William's determination for war, and suggested that John leave immediately if he wanted to be safe. But John felt it was his duty to inform the chief of the situation before he could leave. So he sent a messenger to Shenge with the report of what he had heard. When the Chief received the message, he wrote a letter to William, asking him about his intentions—Peace or War? Willie S. Caulker, the cabinet maker, son of George Stephen II and the chief's nephew, volunteered to deliver the letter. But on his way, to Mambo, he encountered the war boys marching towards Shenge. When they discovered that he was a Caulker of Shenge district, he was captured and would have been killed, if William had not given prior instructions not to kill any Caulkers captured. They were to be brought to him instead. In addition, fortunately for Willie, he had been helpful to William during his trouble in 1878, and his mother had also been kind to him. So he was taken to William's new headquarters, in a place called Gbahongah, where he was set free. Unfortunately by that time, Willie could not return to Shenge because it was no longer safe to travel.

By now the chief was feeling very confused. He had not heard from his friends in the Colonial Government even though he had sent reports of the events at Larwahnah and of William's war preparations at Mambo. Of course he had also not received William's message since Willie had not returned. Feeling totally abandoned and on his own, he decided that he would not run for his life. He preferred to stay where he was instead of seeking refuge any where else. For a while, things seemed to settle down. In fact, from May 27th to June 16th all was quiet and those who had gone away as refugees, returned to their homes.

The War at Shenge

William's war boys, led by their head warrior Combay, advanced towards Shenge. He had told them that, if they captured Shenge, he wanted the head of Thomas Neale Caulker, the left hand and right breast of his wife Sophia Neale Caulker and the head of Rev. Gomer (whom he felt had betrayed him), brought to him. He also wanted the mission destroyed. News soon reached Shenge that the war boys had arrived and were plundering, taking captives and killing at random. When they arrived at the mission Rev Wilberforce's head warrior (Oatah Agbaray) was there with twelve policemen ammunition and a few other well armed men. The war boys came with a white cloth tied to a stick—a sign of peace, and through an interpreter, declared that they were for peace not war. They were told to come nearer if they were for peace, but they did not move. Instead, one of the war boys took a shot at the men on the verandah of the mission house. A few minutes later, another shot was fired, and the war was on.

It was a brutal war between those who were defending the mission (the mission boys) and William's war boys. But the mission boys prevailed and the war boys fled. They were chased and shot. That Sunday, Rev. Gomer ordered the church bell to be rung, but Rev. Wilberforce suggested that the service be held there in case the war boys returned. After the service an attempt was made to bury one of their own who had been shot, but the war boys did return and tried to attack them. However the mission boys were ready. They ended up chasing the war boy who were trying to run away with the loot they had collected. But the loot was too bulky to run with, and had to be thrown away.

A second battle began at Mo Tucker, in which both the policemen and mission warriors were once more fighting against the war boys. It began, to rain, as soon as the fighting began, but they fought on in spite of it. Tommy, one of the mission men, was shot, but was merely grazed. The man who shot him was instantly shot down by another mission man, Lahsiu, who was a faithful servant of Franklyn Caulker. William Caulker's men lost ground as many of them had been shot. The mission warriors and policemen had the advantage because of the rain and the war boys had no choice but to retreat. This time they were chased to Tresmmah and most of them were fatally wounded. When the mission boys who had gone on the chase returned, they found a few war boys still hiding in deserted houses. Farmah Gbondo, one of the mission warriors met one of them and they engaged in a hand to hand fight. The war boy fought very well, and was able to land what could have been a mortal blow on Farmah Gbondo's head, but with good native medicine he was saved. Following this incident, the people in the mission house became extremely vigilant and posted spies at all the dormer windows of the mission house.

The war boys found that it was now difficult to move in pairs, so they spread out in a line on the beach, which was about fifty yards away. Here, they taunted the mission boys with very abusive language, and challenged them to come down and meet them. This went on for about twenty minutes. Meanwhile, a column of the mission boys, was trying to get behind the war boys, so that they could surround them. One of the volunteers at the mission fired a shot, which was returned by the war boys, signaling that they were ready to fight. At that same moment they saw the column of mission boys approaching and tried to run away, but many of them were laden with loot. These items were so bulky, that they found it difficult to carry them while running. By the time they reached N'carthy, they had thrown much of it away. The mission boys collected the plundered goods and returned to Shenge.

Two days later, Captain Halkett from the naval cruiser, came ashore, accompanied by his launch pilots, and fifty policemen. After they settled down, they listened as George Domingo gave them a list of the ring leaders of the war and told them where they could be found. Thomas Kugba Caulker II, William Caulker, Kene Fumoh, and Murana Crimebah were named. When the captain asked how he knew this, George told him that he was there when the chief told some of the section chiefs how he had tried to dissuade William from waging war. Policemen went through the district and arrested all those who had been named. They also recovered some of the Creole captives and sent them to Freetown.

Results and Experiences of the War — The Stories

The war had indeed brought a lot of destruction, from Bendu, all the way in land to Bompeh Candor. There are many stories of the devastation which the war boys brought to the Shenge district and its environs. For the purposes of this book, only a few have been narrated.

At Bompetoke, about forty people were taken captive. Although the town itself was not burned down, a woman named Conyah Boye, her two children and an elderly lady were taken captive and the town was plundered. Mr. J.N. Lefevre a trader had just died, and left his factory to his relative Moses Lefevre. The factory contained cotton goods, hardware, alcohol, tobacco, and rice. There were also many bulls in the compound. The war boys commandeered all the goods and set the factory up as their garrison, and Moses had to leave. While he was gone, he took it upon himself to go and seek out other refugees from Bompetoke, so he traveled around to the surrounding areas. One day he was coming from the town of Thombay, when he met a fourteen year old girl, named Kafway Nassy, in one of the towns. She said the war boys had tried to chase her, but she was such a fast runner, they could not catch up with her. She hid under some bushes, and stayed there for three days only coming out of her hiding place when she saw him.

There is the story of Mr. A.J.Campbell. Mr. J. Arthur Richards who was the pastor in Bompetoke, had just returned from Bonthe, when he realized that he was in danger. He tried to escape by boat but unfortunately, the tide was out and he could not leave immediately. The war boys saw his property in the boat and seized it, but lucky for him, they allowed him to go. When the tide came in he left the mission in the care of Mr. A.J.Campbell, a very unscrupulous man, who got on well with the war boys because he pretended to be a Creole man and the war boys trusted him. (In those days the Creoles were known as Sierra Leoneans). When the boys returned from their plundering, they gave him a share of their loot and in return he gave them tobacco and other things. Some of the refugees who were hiding in the bush would come out at night, sleep in the mission quarters, then creep stealthily back to the bush to hide in the early hours of the morning. Some of them even brought their property to Mr. Campbell for safe keeping. If he was questioned by the war boys he pretended that it was his property.

William Caulker, who was at his headquarters at Gbahongah at the time, wrote letters to some of his friends in England. He gave them to his wife Member, who was to take them to Bonthe to be posted. To make the trip, Member disguised herself as a refugee. On the way, she stopped at Mr. A.F. Campbell's home in Bompetoke. Since they were friends, she shared her secret with him. She told him that she was going to Bonthe to post some letters from William. She then gave them to Campbell for safe keeping. The crooked man secretly read the letters and when he found out whom they were for, and that they were complaints against the Colony, he removed them from the envelopes and replaced them with blank paper. Unknown to her, Member continued on to Bonthe with what were now bogus letters. After Member left, one of the war boys came to see Campbell, and noticed that the size of his property seemed to have increased. There were several more boxes around. Campbell tried to tell them that he had brought the boxes down from upstairs to sort them out. But when he turned his back, some of the war boys noticed marks on his neck which they immediately recognized as Poro markings. Campbell pleaded with them, saying that his mother was a Temne woman and his father was a Creole, but they refused to listen. They ordered him to go outside and prepare for death. Within minutes, everything in the house had been taken, Campbell was stripped of his clothing and taken outside. He was only allowed to take his Bible with him as he was marched to the spot where he would be executed. He asked if he could take a little time to pray and they agreed. After the prayer, as they sang a war song, they marched him to the execution spot. Just as they were ready to execute him, a man came and asked them to hold off on the execution until they had conferred with their General, Mormor Margbah who also claimed to be a Creole and had orders not to kill any Creole. Mormor knew Campbell well, since he was tutoring his brother Ali. He quickly gave the order not to kill Campbell, and thus saved his life.

William Caulker's Downfall

William had a mistress, Charlotte Hingston, who had been living with him as his wife during the war. She gained many benefits for her business from this association. Trading in such commodities as palm oil and kola nuts, made her a very rich woman. When the war ended, she talked William into getting her a boat so she could go to Freetown to sell her produce. This he did, but when she arrived in Freetown, she immediately went to the police and told Mr. Lawson where William could be found. William was captured in the town of Gbawonga. His cousin Thomas Kugba, Murana Crimebah (a.k.a Karimu), a man called Lahai, and Chief Richard Canreba Caulker were also arrested. But William knew the prosecutor well. It was none other than Sir Samuel Lewis, (who had defended him in a previous trial) who had since been knighted and was now the Crown Prosecutor.

The trial began on January 17th 1888 and lasted until May 1st. The final speech to the jury took three days to deliver. In the end, William, his cousin Thomas Kugba and Lahai, were found guilty of murder. The jury recommended mercy, but the government wanted to make examples of them. The gallows were set up in Shenge near the shore and William Thomas George Caulker of Mambo, Thomas Kugba Caulker of Shenge and Lahai, were hanged in May 1888.

Public sympathy was with William, because he had ordered his men not to kill Creoles. Many from the colony believed that if the government had enforced English law in Shenge which was considered a British territory, this would not have happened. William was seen as the victim of a greedy, irresponsible power, which denied its subjects the protection of law, then punished them when they took matters into their own hands.

The account of the execution was carried in the weekly newspaper, and described how William forgave his enemies, and how women stood watching the three gallows from a distance. This they reported, introduced similarities with the story of the crucifixion. This report was underlined by another commentary which talked about 'Divine retribution visited on Jerusalem'.

Four of William's supporters including his cousin Richard Canreba Caulker, were deported to the Gambia. Richard was told that he was being sent to the Gambia, to meditate in exile on the tarnished glories of the House of Caulker. *(Fyfe 1993)*

* * *

3. The Caulkers and the Hut Tax War.

In 1894, Colonel Frederick Cardew, arrived in Freetown to replace Governor Sir Francis Flemming who was ill. Within a few weeks, the new governor made a six week tour of the country. As he traveled, he wondered about the best way to turn an area which was British on paper, but was still ruled by sovereign chiefs, into a full fledged British protectorate. If the area were fully annexed, he would have to introduce 'English law' to people who knew nothing about it, and then try to enforce the law. He did not really want to do that. So he decided it would be best to introduce a form of 'Indirect Rule'. This way the chiefs would be allowed to continue ruling, but would be 'assisted' and therefore limited by European District Commissioners. By the end of the 19th Century, the British had annexed much of the area outside the colony, and had acquired jurisdiction in all the chiefdoms which were around the colony. These chiefdoms were referred to as, "Foreign countries adjoining the Colony".

In 1896, the Protectorate was established over the area which the British had claimed, and Governor Cardew now had to develop policies for ruling the area. But he needed money to pay for this new administration and the British Government was insisting that the money should be raised locally. As he traveled around the country, Cardew came up with several ideas on how to resolve his dilemma. Among them, was the idea of levying direct taxes in the Protectorate. He thought, the people would pay ten shillings on houses with four rooms, and five shillings on houses with fewer rooms. He then decided that the chiefs would be responsible for collecting the taxes from their subjects in return for a commission of three pence per house. Unfortunately, Cardew underestimated the stiff opposition he would face from the people in the Protectorate, when he presented his tax proposal. Arrogantly, he traveled around telling the people about the coming tax. They received the news politely and often said nothing. The governor misconstrued their reaction to the news and thought that their protests were being instigated by Creole agitators. Some of the chiefdoms were so upset, they sent petitions to Freetown. Chief Be Sherbro of Yoni, even got Poro to prohibit the sale of produce to Europeans and Creoles, thinking they were responsible fo this new tax. Since the government could not have him arrested, they devised a way to detain him if it became necessary. They passed a rule which made it a crime to use Poro to restrain trade. With this new rule, the Poro chiefs lost control over their produce—a power which they had previously been able to exercise. (Fyfe 1964)

Richard Canreba Caulker of Bompeh, who had been exiled to the Gambia following William's trial in 1888, was reinstated in 1894. At first, he forbade his people to pay the taxes, but he suddenly changed his mind and began to collect them. Governor Cardew though, suspected that Richard was associated with another chief, Bai Kompa of Bombali and that they were in some scheme together. So he had Richard arrested and jailed in Kwelu. The governor's suspicions were correct, for while he was incarcerated, Richard did admit that although he had paid ten pounds in tax, he had sent seventy pounds to Koinadugu, where the government could not find it.

In 1896, the governor paid a visit to Shenge to explain the tax rules. But Aunty Lucy—(the first United Brethren Church convert) advised her half brother, chief Thomas Neale Caulker, to refuse to pay the tax. The chief did not pay any attention to her. He knew that many of his subjects still thought of him as a usurper and his late cousin, William of Mambo, was a martyr. Infact, he had been warned against enforcing the tax and there were rumors going around, that if he made his people pay a tax, there would be war. But Thomas Neale-Caulker, was loyal to the government because, he felt that they had appointed him chief and had supported his administration. So he was determined to uphold the tax ruling no matter what his subjects were saying. Two members of the Frontier Force, were sent from the Colony to help Thomas Neale collect the taxes. As the soldiers went around, they ruthlessly demanded instant payment. They tied up anyone who refused to pay, and burned their homes. They created a lot of havoc as they attempted to collect the taxes, but ended up collecting two thousand pounds from Roinetta District, which covered Bompeh and Shenge /Plantain districts.

The Governor was furious that the some of the chiefs were resisting his edict about paying taxes, and sent soldiers around the country. Unfortunately, while the soldiers collected the tax revenue, they also cultivated bitter hatred. So an uprising was planned by the chiefs and their people. The planners used Poro to ensure secrecy. When the appointed day for the uprising dawned, messengers were sent throughout the country with a burnt palm leaf as the signal. The town of Bumpe in Mende country, was designated the central point.

On April 27 1896, the attack began. Given the accumulated grievances against the government for its methods of tax collection, those who hated the Creoles, the missionaries and the unpopular chiefs, broke into a wave of fury which spread over the country. It seemed as if the people were trying to rid the country of all alien influence. They dredged up every wrong or perceived wrong they could think of. They actually wanted to drive the Europeans into the sea. The Vai, Bullom, Loko, Mabenta and Temnes joined the fight. All aliens, that is, all Europeans or Creoles, or anyone who had anything to do with them,—their wives, their employees or those whom they had educated, were the targets. A few people had been warned in advance and had gone into hiding. But a man was killed near Shenge, because he had been caught helping some Creoles to escape. *(Fyfe 1993)*

Undercover of the general massacre, the Caulkers had their own drama.

As the war came closer to Shenge, Rev. L. Bartner, the missionary in charge of the Shenge mission, called, Mr. Alphonso T. Caulker, who at the time was a teacher and boarding home master at the Rufus Clarke school, and instructed him to prepare the mission boats. He was to choose a few able bodied boys who could ferry the mission boys and girls across to Kent. There were 25 boys and 16 girls in all, and there were four mission boats available—*The Olive branch*, the *Salem*, the *Flickinger* and *the Messenger*. The women and children were taken to Plantain island and Mr. AT Caulker, who captained *the Olive Branch*, took the boarders directly to Kent. The remaining students were also taken to Plantain Island in *the Messenger* and later joined their friends in Kent. Eventually, they were all taken to Kent. Rev. Bartner tried to persuade Thomas Neale to escape with him, but Thomas refused to go. He said that he would await his retribution in his own chiefdom. So the missionaries, Rev.and Mrs. L.O. Bartner, Rev. and Mrs. F.S. Misshall and baby Lois, all boarded *the Flickinger* and *the Salem* and crossed over to Kent.

The attack on Shenge was led by Alexander P. Doomabey, whose surname caused everyone to remember the wickedness of his father, the former chief of Mando. Alexander Doomabey had been educated by the United Brethren in Christ (UBC) missionaries and had worked as their accountant. He had also been a candidate for the ministry, but due to a quarrel with the missionaries, as is so often the case, he bore them a grudge. When the signal for the attack came, Alex threw off his coat and trousers, wore an ancestral headdress and led the party which attacked and sacked the Shenge Mission, and killed all who were still there. (*Fyfe 1993*)

In the meantime, Francis Caulker of Mambo, who was still bent on avenging his brother William's death, saw this confusion as his chance to go in search of the chief. The chief and two of his sons had hidden on a small secluded island behind the forest at Tasso. No one knew of this place except the chiefdom speaker Gbana Bome, the chief's right hand man. One can speculate that Gbana Bome had made contact with Francis Caulker's boys and made an arrangement with them, or like everyone else in the chiefdom, he did not like his chief who was particularly unpopular at this time.

While the war boys searched for the chief, Gbana Bome was paying a little visit to his chief at his hiding place. He pretended he was there to have a confidential talk. They spoke for a while and when he was ready to leave, the chief gave him some oranges for his journey. As he walked towards town, Gbana Bome began to peel and eat the oranges throwing the peels on the ground. On his way, he met war boys who asked if he knew where the chief was hiding. Gbana Bome did not hesitate to betray his chief. He told the boys to follow the orange peels if they wanted to find his hiding place. The boys followed his instructions, found the chief, assassinated him, but spared his sons.

And so, the chief's cousin, Francis Caulker of Mambo, (this writer's great-grandfather), got his revenge on the so called 'slave born usurper.

Due to Chief Thomas Neale's loyalty to the British government, at his death the chief's staff was given to his wife Sophia Neale-Caulker in 1898. *(Tower)*

The End of the War

Eventually, the Hut Tax war was brought under control with the help of naval vessels. Governor Cardew declared that every chief was responsible for the uprising, but in the end only six chiefs were implicated. The Governor also began his new policy of using the chiefs to administer the Protectorate. A few of the chiefs were recognized as those on whom the Government could depend. These included Madam Yoko, Nancy Tucker, James Canreba Caulker of Bompeh and Madam Sophia Neale-Caulker, of Shenge/Plantain, who represented George Stephen I (Ba Charch) line by birth and the Thomas Stephen (Ba Tham) line by marriage. With their help the Protectorate was restored. *(Fyfe 1962)*

After the war, there was no longer a large settlement at Plantain Island. Sherbro fishermen went there to fish and three individuals, Madam Mary.G. Caulker, commonly called Aunty Pappy or Yemi Pappy, Mr. Garnet Wolsley, commonly called Ba Garnet, and Madam Eva P. Caulker (commonly called Yemi Hota) continued farming there. Foni Vil, a tenant of Aunty Pappy, who worked as her caretaker, and took care of her pigs was the first Sherbro to build a hut on the island after the war. Probably due to Mary Caulker's status as a family elder in the community, She subsequently became the sole custodian of Plantain Island. *(Tower)*

Part IV

The Ancestors and their Influence

Chapter IX

The Ancestors and their influence

Africans have always had ancient and well established traditions—a way of thinking and a way of living. These traditions cannot easily be thrown out, just because someone comes along, and says *"Our way is the better way. You must give up all your traditions, your culture and all you have ever known and become Christian"*. *(Colin Turnbul)—The Lonely African.*

Giving up one's culture and traditions, especially on a stranger's say so is very difficult to do. Yet, this is exactly what the European and American Missionaries were demanding when they arrived to 'civilize the heathens.' For our ancestors, this must have been an outrage, especially as these men and women, from a family of chiefs who had been independent agents all of their lives, were now being asked not only to give up their identity, their integrity and their pride, but to make their people do the same, in order to follow some strangers' dictates. This must have been a source of great consternation and great resentment. In fact, we do know that Chief Thomas Stephen of Shenge/Plantain chiefdom, refused to have anything to do with the missionaries when they first arrived.

The colonialists and the missionaries demanded that converted Africans wear western clothes, assume western names and adapt to western thinking, manners and customs, if they wanted to be viewed as Christians. In other words, they were to divest themselves of their African identity, in much the same way the slaves who had been shipped away, had been forced to do when they arrived on the plantations.

The Caulkers of Sierra Leone

In the newly formed Colony of Freetown, those who had come fom England, America, Canada and the Caribbean, had arrived as freed slaves with their new western ideas, and already understood that they had to start of thinking of themselves as a new nation. rather than simply as being from a tribe. They understood that they were now one people, here to build a colony. On the other hand, the recaptured slaves who had been returned before they were taken into slavery, were now caught in the middle. They had come from other parts of West Africa, and had not experienced the full impact of slavery on their lives. So their original traditions and cultures were still in tact. But they too, had to change their tribal way of thinking, as they adjusted to the western ways in the new colony.

As the western ways took a hold in the colony, the chiefs and their people in Sierra Leone's hinterland, where the tribal norms were stronger, had to make a choice between maintaining the old traditions or changing to a new way of life. These choices were not so much about economics or politics, but rather, they were about protecting the soul of their people—their hopes, their fears, their emotions and their relationships. *(Colin Turnbul) The Lonely African.*

One can see that this was a dilemma which our ancestors had to face.—a situation which pulled them in different directions. They knew that if they were to go forward, they would have to give up a past, in which the roots of their very being were nourished. But if they were to go backward they would be giving up on the promises of the future. *(Colin Turnbul)—The Lonely African*

Given their origins as Euro-Africans, the early Caulkers and other Afro-Europeans, did not have a problem adjusting to western cultural norms. After all, they had European fathers and European (Christian names) and had interacted with Europeans over the years. But by the mid 19th century, things had begun to change. The hinterland was slowly being annexed and British flags were being hoisted all over the land. Missionaries from America and England had arrived, looking to convert 'The Heathens'. African Sovreignty was slowly coming to a close, and the power of the chiefs was slowly being diminished. Life as they had known it was beginning to look and feel different.

For later generations of Caulkers, life had indeed changed. Whilst many of the ancestors had been light skinned, later generations tended to be darker than their parents, who had married people from within Sierra Leone and other parts of West Africa. Their education was primarily in the local schools which had been built and run by missionaries, or in the new colony of Freetown, where many of them got their secondary education. They were now faced with the problem of how to maintain their status and integrity as the leaders of their people, the representatives of their culture and proud African men and women. Drawing from their Euro-African heritage and their indigenous culture, they understood the value of education. As George Caulker of Mambo, this writer's grandfather, said when he scribbled his thoughts on 'the importance of education'on a scrap of paper, dated March 29th 1932: *"If a man is able to think and speak and act in a more advanced way than others because of his education, he must also serve his country. God rewards such a one in various ways. He bestows on him the blessing of the ability to do more and more".* So, they used their training to teach their people the benefits of having the best of both worlds. They led by example.

They understood the new colonial law—British Law, but most often ruled their people using customary law. They continued their relationships with Muslims and Christians alike, and many of them, like Francis Caulker of Mambo,(author's great grandfather), gave their girls in marriage to Muslim traders and raised their sons as Christians. This created a Christian/Moslem family, where family relationships and values came first at all times. But above all, they made sure all their children got an education.

In the mid 19th century, there were two important cultural issues which the ancestors had to deal with. First was Polygamy, and the second was membership in the the Poro institution. The missionaries viewed both of these as 'pagan' practices, and strongly discouraged them. But giving them up was especially difficult for those in a ruling family. In the case of polygamy, as rulers they often received new wives from various regions, as a way of establishing alliances. To return the gift would have been an insult to the giver. So they married their new wives according to customary law and had children by them. The belief was that a man's wealth could be counted by the number of children he had, and the number of people he had around him. But one wife was the principal wife—the head wife, and this union was blessed by the missionaries whenever possible. This was probably a concession to their Christian training and their beliefs,

In the case of the Poro Institution, the Caulkers of Bompeh had become Poro members well before the Shenge/Plantain Caulkers. But after the terrible experience Thomas Stephen had before the onset of the war with Canreba Caulker, he established a Poro bush in Shenge. Hence most of the Caulker men became members of the poro institution. Membership in Poro, gave access to all parts of the country, and initiated members, were seen as adult men.(Remember James Cleveland, son of William Cleveland, who joined Poro to enhance his position of power in the 1700's.)

Non-initiated men were viewed as children and were subjected to being in the house, clapping with the women when the Poro spirit was around—a very demeaning role for a man.

Thomas Stephen Caulker thought Poro was the equivalent of the Masonic Lodge. *(Fyfe)—History*. This statement was of interest to me, since my father Dr. Richard Kelfa-Caulker told me he joined the Lodge, so that he could compare it to Poro. When I asked what he thought about his experiences he said, "Poro is light years ahead of the Lodge. There is no comparison". At his death in 1975, thanks to his brother and cousins present (all Poro members), Poro was very much a part of the Wake in Freetown, much to the consternation of those Krios present. To me this demonstrated my father's dilemma.

Living in a time when becoming a Christian meant giving up almost everything African, the choice of having to give up membership in Poro or not, was a difficult one to make. Between ages 9 and 10, male children joined Poro, either before they went to school, or during their first year in school. Once members, they were in for good and their membership could not be taken away. Hence, the ancestors maintained their cultural beliefs and not only remained Poro members, but made sure that their sons followed the tradition, in order that they too would be seen as powerful adult men.

Many of the Caulker men had been educated at the Rufus Clark and Wife school in Shenge, while some of the women went to the Mary Sowers school in Rotifunk. When the Harford School and the Albert Academy opened, many went there for the secondary school education.

Since their learning experiences had been run mostly by the missionaries, some chose careers in the ministry, whilst others became teachers. Many Caulker men also travelled to other parts of the country, either to teach and/or be pastors in remote churches. Some of them took on roles in the colonial government and assisted in establishing the Protectorate council.

Probably, because of their European background or their interaction with the missionaries, they had been exposed to classical music as well as local music. Indeed, many were musicians in their own right, playing a variety of instruments including the concertina and accordion. Most, never had formal music lessons, but they played beautifully by ear. Singing was simply a family tradition which most Caulkers still enjoy. I remember, each time we visited our grandparents in Mambo, a requirement was to learn a song from the Sankey hymnal. My grandfather, playing his harmonium, practiced with us, so that we could perform our song during a service. (Services were held in the living room.) My grandmother sang all the songs by memory!!

But in spite of their mission school experiences and their leadership roles in the colonial government, Caulker men stuck to their convictions and stood tall as men from the Protectorate. They were the leaders in their families and in their communities, a role which they took seriously.

The women on the other hand, did not always have the opportunities for travel which the men had, but they were not limited. They were the backbone of the family. They knew all that was happening in the family and the chiefdom. Their fingers were on the pulse of their villages and the chiefdom, and they often provided guidance for the men. Some of them were the midwives of the village, and they helped to deal with various health issues.

Although a few Caulker women were members of the Bundu society, (like the Poro, an institution of learning for girls), interestingly, many were not initiated. !" One reason I am told, is that many Caulker women were educated and understood the dangers of some of the rites of the society. Another reason was that they tended to have relationships with their male cousins (often distantly related) who were not only educated but very good looking, and they did not have to deal with the sexual issues and attitudes commonly encountered with the uneducated and/or 'foreign' men.

In my experience, during my childhood, I recall feeling like an outsider whenever we travelled to the village and I was among those who had been initiated. Once, during a visit to Mambo for Christmas, I remember begging my grandmother to allow me to join, so that I could be like my playmates who were preparing for the junior Bundu parade in the village. But she sternly informed me "Caulker women do not join Bundu". I recall my tears and my disappointment!!! At the ripe old age of 8, I envied my village friends and relatives for their beautiful beads around their necks and hips, their colorful wraps and headties, and their dark skins glowing with oil. As they danced to the beat of the drums, under a canopy, carried by the adult members. How I wished I could have joined them! (Author)

The Caulker women raised not only their own children, but also took in many children whose parents, many of whom came from other parts of the chiefdom, brought their children for education and training. In their new home, the children learned the art of cooking and how to perform other household chores. It was always interesting to watch the woman of the house, sit under a large tree in front of the kitchen, directing the children in meal preparation. The women also felt responsible for every child who crossed their path, and were free to punish any child who made the unfortunate mistake of misbehaving in front of one of them. They were the disciplinarians! *"There is the story of a child (Aunty Mildred) who was running towards the beach in Shenge one day. On her way she passed 'Aunty Pappy's house. In her haste she yelled out a greeting—"Cousin Pappy n'saka"—"Good morning cousin Pappy". The insult was that she had referred to this family elder as 'cousin' instead of 'Aunty'. Needless to say, on her way back, the unsuspecting child was called in to Aunty Pappy's house, and thinking she was going to get a treat, went eagerly. For her trouble, she got a slap on her bottom for 'insulting an elder'. This was a lesson she never forgot."* (as told by Mildred Caulker)

It must be noted here that Aunty Pappy, whose real name was Mrs. Mary Gomer French, was not someone to be trifled with. It is said she was a formidable woman, who was one of the tribal authorities. When she spoke, her voice could be heard a long distance away. She owned a farm on Plantain Island, and raised poultry, pigs and goats.

It is important to note here, that there was as much love given out as there was discipline.

These mothers, aunts and grandmothers, were also the backbone of the church. By their example, they made sure all the children in their care went to Sunday School and church. If a child got sleepy during the service, the punishment was to stand for the remainder of the service. They could sing every hymn, and recite every bible verse from memory, so it was easy to monitor the children who were also expected to sing as loudly as they could. They were always an important part of the welcoming committee. When a visitor arrived, they made sure food was prepared and sent for the guest. They sent vegetables, fruit, oil, new rice, or fish for the guest. The 'girls' in the house prepared baths, and generally made the visitor comfortable. The women were the entrepreneurs. They raised and sold anything from vegetables to some livestock. They visited the homes of their siblings and cousins on a regular basis, often travelling by boat or simply walking, since in their day, there were no cars. They attended any family event that came up—funerals, weddings, or births, often being part of the planning and execution of these events. They were also available as family cousellors, settling marital quarrels or other family issues. They were strong women who, probably, to the chagrin of the men, simply 'took over' without giving the men a chance to participate.

Indeed, the women in the family did not seem to pay too much attention to real or perceived rifts. In fact, there are those who may dispute the idea of rifts within the family, thanks to the great influence of the Caulker women. As far as they were concerned, family is family, no matter what. They made sure that for their children, there would be little to no differentiation between the family branches. They visited family where ever they happened to be. Fortunately even today, this sense of 'family' has persisted through the years and has allowed us to gather for various family occasions, and at least voice the understanding that 'we are one family'.

The women have also played a major role, both as leaders in their communities and as matriarchs in their families. Our earliest ancestor, Queen Yema Cumba was Queen of Tasso in the early 1700's, and it is likely that one of her relatives was one of the signatories during the purchase of land by the British for the newly arrived freed slaves. In 1898, Madam Sophia Neale-Caulker became paramount chief of the Plantain Shenge chiefdom, and Madam Honoria Bailor-Caulker became chief of Kagboro in 1962. Most recently, Madam Doris Lenga-Caulker Gbabior II became chief of Kagboro in 2010. Many Caulker women also became teachers in the girls' schools and some later served in the government. In 1985, the late Mrs. Amelia Ben-Davis (nee Caulker) of Mambo House was made a Member of Parliament, The late Mrs Patricia Kabba, grand daughter of Charles Caulker of Mambo House, demonstrated an impressive example of leadership as First Lady of the Republic of Sierra Leone, between 1996 and her untimely death in 1998. There are many unsung female heroes who have not been mentioned. Indeed Caulker women continue to show remarkable strength no matter where they find themselves.

These were the men and women who carried the beacon of their ancestors and passed it on to us. Now we must pass it on to the next generation.

Chapter X

The Last Word

The Author's notes

As I draw this book to a close, it seems to me that the question "What is our Heritage," should be addressed one more time, this time by the Caulker youth of today.

After a few Family Reunions, this is what the young people said about their Heritage

My heritage as a Caulker

As a member of the younger generation of Caulkers, in the past, whenever I heard the elders talking of the family and how proud they were, I would say to myself, "Oh, there they go again!!" or "not again, like we have not heard that Caulker Heritage story a thousand time before!"

But I tell you, now more than ever, I want to hear that story, over and over and over again. What I am referring to extends beyond a symbol like the family crest or beyond tribal sentiments. As I contemplate why my heritage as a Caulker is significant in present day Sierra Leone, I have come to realize that, in light of the recent war in Sierra Leone, for me, the "Caulker Heritage" discussion has now taken on a different meaning.

The word 'Heritage' means, what has been or will be inherited. "I am a Caulker". To me, my 'Heritage' means, whether I like it or not, that I am a descendant of an old line of chiefs and other extremely prominent people who have served Sierra Leone honorably in various capacities. There have been Caulkers in government, civic, social and in fact all facets of the Sierra Leone community. Bur we keep asking ourselves questions like 'What happened to Sierra Leone?' How?, Why?.

A country's most valuable resource is its people. Let us seize the opportunity to continue what those who came before us started, but left for us to finish. I cannot just sit down and be satisfied with that statement *"I am a Caulker"*, and expect to be showered with love, affection and or prosperity. To me, the statement *"I am a Caulker"* means responsibility. The responsibility of propagating what the ancestors were able to do, in a way that benefits present day society. There is the responsibility of teaching family members our history so that we get a sense of where we came from and where we are heading as a family . . . We will not know what we are capable of unless we try—TOGETHER. Just uttering those words *"I am a Caulker"*, builds confidence in my heart, because I know I am never alone.

We do bear the burden of rebuilding our nation—It is time we buckle down and take control of our home land, otherwise somebody else will be telling us what to do with it.

Having this Heritage means, that we can work together, to bring our dreams to the realm of reality.

By Richard Bai Bangura
Great Grandson of PC A.T. Caulker of Kagboro Chiefdom

On Caulker Women

I was proud and happy when the Caulker Descendants Family Reunion came to Atlanta in 2000. I made plans ahead of time to meet some of my extended family for the first time. I was excited to learn about the richness of the Caulker Family history. I was especially happy to learn that the Caulker women have always played and are still playing important roles in their communities, as mothers, friends, leaders, advisors, spokeswomen and overall role models. It is these examples of feminine strength that I gladly received.

Lango Barlay
—Great granddaughter of PC A.G. Caulker of Bompeh Chiefdom

As a Caulker woman, being at this family reunion, I think back to the memories of visiting my grandmother, Gladys, in Shenge and Bompetoke. To a child, this was just another fun road trip with family—A chance to play on the hot white sand, and swim on the clear blue sea water.... Today, those memories represent a lot more that a good time. They remind me that I am in a land which is not my home. They remind me that no matter how many countries I visit or how many people I meet, in the end, all that matters is family. It is having a past, having deep roots and a strong heritage to look back on with pride. The Caulker family is full of women who are beautiful examples of what I want to be.

Caulker women are strong spirited, warm, generous and giving. I have seen many hold their heads up high while life dealt them blow after blow. I have seen them give love unselfishly, when no one was loving them back. I have seen them maintain their sense of humor in times when life gave them little to smile about. I look up to all these role models—aunties, cousins, sisters, grandmas, as beacons of light in my times of darkness.

We are a new generation of Caulker daughters and we have nothing but great women to look up to—women of courage, pioneering, innovative, leaders, academicians, They have achieved all sorts of accomplishments with a deep sense of pride and dignity in their ancestry.

I see Caulker women walk with their heads held high, with regal bearing.
I try to walk that way.
I see Caulker women laugh with joy when surrounded by family
I want to laugh with them.
I see Caulker women setting examples in all facets of lie
And I want to follow them.

Tanya Bangura
—Great granddaughter of PC. A.T. Caulker of Kagboro Chiefdom

Indeed, the Caulker family is one with several unique qualities which are threaded throughout its history. It is a family which has tried to maintain its African culture in spite of its strong western beginnings. But what, you might ask, is African Culture?

An Ancestor discusses African Culture.

In a speech given on African Culture Day 1970 in Liberia, the late Dr. Richard E.Kelfa-Caulker talked about what is meant by 'maintaining the African Culture'.

"I was born a Bullom, of the oldest tribe in Sierra Leone. I knew not a word of English until I was sent to the Mission school at Shenge at the age of ten. At age twelve, I was sent home to be initiated into the Poro Institution along with y brothers and other boys of my age. We learned the Poro songs and dances and learned to beat the drums. I became a champion drummer. My parents were Christians when they came together, so they introduced us to Christianity. They tried to bring us up in the Christian tradition, but it was not until I was twelve that I became a member of the United Brethren Church and. was baptized.

African Culture can be appreciated primarily in the African Secret Societies. For us,(Bulloms) the two major ones are The Poro Institution, for the men and the Bundu or Sandi, for the women. There are other minor ones which are limited to particular tribes. Some specialize in certain areas such as government, law, war, medicine, farming and so on. These societies were and are, for most Africans, truly an educational system. But other people came—the missionaries brought with them Western Education and Religion as well as the whole panoply of what we now have and practice. From this point on, we could no longer talk of 'African Culture. Our habits and our language began to change. Now, we find we can express ourselves more widely and completely in the basic languages of English, French, German and others.

But while we may not quite know where we are going, let us not forget where we have come from.

Evidence of our culture may be seen in our carvings and sculpture, our songs and dances and the clothes we weave and wear. Also, in the many different knds of mats and baskets that we make. The Bulloms are referred to in history as famous for carving ivory objects, making wooden combs and masques for spirit dancers. I recall a man in our village, who made beautiful ladies combs and hair parters. He also carved head masques for the Spirit dances.

These masques or spirit heads are erroneously called devils, such as Bundu devils or Poro devils. The word 'devil' is an importation from England and America. Africans do not have the word 'devil' in their vocabulary. They have the word Spirit. Thus there are good spirits and bad spirits. I suspect that the word or idea of 'the devil' was imported to Africa by Christian missionaries who, in their endeavour to find an excuse for coming to Africa, condemned everything African and called it evil. They created the 'devil'. In some places, they even changed our African names, gave us western names which they called "Christian names". We now give those names to our children.

Now, the masques which our people made and wore, and were daubed 'Devil heads', are very much sought after by English and American and other European scholars. Yet we have been taught to call them devils and we teach our children to call them devils. Thus we talk of the Poro devil instead of the Poro spirit. When the Bulloms refer to the Holy Spirit, they do not mean 'devil' the sherbro phrase "Min Charang de" simply means "Clean Spirit".

We ought therefore to set the record straight by using the correct words when we Africans use or translate words into English or vice versa. It will help us and the foreigners, to appreciate our African Culture better.

Let us cultivate African Culture, for culture is a growing thing. It is a continuing thing. Let us encourage our carvers, weavers and basket makers. Let us patronize our African Culture, let us sing and tell African stories. It is a way of educating our children. It is African. Let us practice and encourage African Culture. We will never become English or American men and women. We are Africans!!!!! (Richard E Kelfa-Caulker)

Our elders have also taught us of our spiritual connection with the ancestors, whom they believe, are always around and act as guardians and mediators with God. Therefore we follow the tradition of recognizing and honoring them at family gatherings. As a family, religion, whether Christianity or Islam, plays a major role in family life. In our family, Christians and Moslems are relatives and live side by side in love and respect for each other. In spite of the apparent family rifts, and thanks to the very strong women in the family, there has always been a sense of family. For instance in the past, during each war, orders were given to the war boys on each side, not to kill Caulker men or to harm Caulker women. After the war with Canreba, a woman in Thomas Stephen's family, talked him into forgiving his nephew Thomas Kugba, whom he had raised, but who had turned against him. Today we continue to have our family squabbles, but we never forget that we are family. We support each other by attending family events joyfully, even in 'ashwebi' if that is the wear.

Caulkers seem to be drawn to positions of responsibility and, many different professions. Some of them have also been called to serve their country, like the late Dr. John Karefa-Smart—Minister of Foreign Affairs,(to name one of his many positions) or service in the Diplomatic Corps, like the late Dr. Richard Kelfa-Caulker—First Ambassador to the USA and UN, Rev. Dr. William Fitzjohn—First High Commisioner to the Court of St. James, Mr. Victor Sumner—First Secretary in the Sierra Leone to the United Nations, Mr. Valecious Caulker—Member of Parliament, Mr. Melvin Challobah—Ambassador to the Court of St. James, and Mrs. Annie Bangura—Principal Officer of Social Affairs, ECOWAS, to name a few. These individuals, have demonstrated the sense of commitment to whatever task they undertake, which is inherent in our heritage.

Yes, we have been given a rich heritage of achievements and role models. The beacon has been passed and the next generation must know the story. Yes they fought bitter battles amongst themselves, but by their example they managed to teach us good things about family unity.

To reiterate the words of Paramount Chief Charles Caulker of Bompeh Chiefdom,

> *"We have been born into royalty and we have a role to play in the development of our country Sierra Leone. Whether one is from Bompeh or from Kagboro, we are first, ONE FAMILY."*

Appendices

Appendix I

Summary of the Caulker Rulers — from 1780-1999

*I*n 1722, the Thomas Corker descendants began their rule after the death of their grandmother Chief Yema Cumba Queen of Tasso, otherwise known as, Senora Doll. While Yema Cumba was alive, her children, Robin (Skinner) and Stephen were made section chiefs. Skinner was section chief of Banana Island, and Stephen as the older son, remained on the main land. These early Corkers carried their paternal name (which later morphed into Caulker) and inherited claim to the chieftaincy from the maternal side of the family. They became known as The Cumba-Corker(Caulkers).

After Chief Yema Cumba's death, her grandson Thomas (Stephen's son) was crowned chief of Old Kagbor, probably in 1723. At the time the Cumba-Corker house was the only recognized ruling house. The area they ruled was known as the Bompeh Kingdom or Greater Kagbor, and was incorporated into Sierra Leone in 1888.

The second Ruling house—Dyebo-Sosant Dick House, became recognized as a ruling house in Kagbor, after the hinterland of Sierra Leone was declared a Protectorate in 1896. Once they were recognized, they had the right to compete for the chieftaincy.

THE CORKER/CAULKERS KINGS

1. **1723—Thomas Corker**—son of Stephen Corker, was crowned chief, after the death of his grandmother Senora Doll (Queen Yema Cumba of Tasso). There is little known or written about his rule, but with a 58 year gap between the beginning of his reign and the beginning of his son Charles' reign, one can speculate that either he ruled for a long time, or that one of his brothers (not named) also ruled either in his own right or as Regent chief. This may be how succession from brother to brother came into being in the Old Kagbor Kingdom.
2. **1780-1785 Charles Corker**—son of Chief Thomas Corker. He ruled for five years, then was beheaded by order of James Cleveland, son of William Clevland.
3. **1785-1795 William Corker**—also a son of Thomas Corker, became chief after his brother's assassination. He was expected to avenge his brother's death. He and his brother Stephen quarreled endlessly over this, and in the end, William died without getting the job done.
4. **1796-1810 Stephen Caulker**—Avenged his brother's death and carried James Cleveland's tombstone to be placed at the entrance to the family burial ground in Tasso. He also reclaimed the Banana Islands which had been taken over by the Clevelands and became known as the "Re-conqueror of the Bananas".
5. **1810-1832 Thomas Kon Tham**—also a son of Thomas Corker, succeeded his brother Stephen. But Stephen's son George Stephen, who had just returned from England, asked his uncle if he would be willing to divide the kingdom so that he could rule a small part of it. Kon Tham agreed and gave George the Plantain islands and Shenge, while he took the Banana islands, where he resided, and the Northern Mainland of the chiefdom (now Bompeh). For the first time, the "Old Kagbor" chiefdom was divided into Bompeh and Plantain/Shenge. Tasso remained the family burial ground.

   In 1820 Kon Tham, was persuaded to lease Banana Islands to the crown, for an annual rent of 250 bars, which was to be paid in Spanish dollars. The bars were valued at 1 bar for each Spanish dollar. Following this transaction, Kon Tham moved to the main land.

The Koya Temne, who had also claimed the Banana Islands, were compensated, and the islands were used to house the recaptured slaves. (those slaves who, on their way to the Americas, had been re-captured on the high seas and were being returned to Freetown). Here, Dublin Village was laid out and built.

So it was, Thomas Kon Tham died in 1832, leaving behind two chiefdoms which made up Old Kagbor.

CHIEFS OF THE DIVIDED 'OLD KAGBOR' CHIEFDOM

THE BOMPEH CAULKER CHIEFS

1. **1832-1842 Charles Caulker**—succeeded his brother Kon Tham as chief. During his rule he opened the country to timber traders. Thus creating a vibrant timber trade on the shores of the Yawry Bay, south of the Colony. He supported his nephew James Canreba Caulker, in his bid to get back the Plantain/Shenge Chiefdom, but he died in 1842, before the end of that war.
2. **1842-1857 James Canreba Caulker**—This son of Thomas Kon Tham, was considered the 'Crown Prince' of Bompeh by his people. He was more popular than his uncle Chief Charles Caulker had been. But it seems he was an angry man! He was angry that his father had divided the chiefdom, and he was angry that the Plantain/Shenge Caulkers had questioned his parentage. So, with support from Chief Charles, he waged war against his cousin Thomas Stephen of Plantain/Shenge, claiming he wanted to reunite the Old Kagbor Chiefdom. At the end of the war, the division of the 'Old Kagbor' chiefdom was made formal by a treaty which was signed in 1845. It stated that Canreba Caulker would rule areas north of the Cockboro Creek and Thomas Stephen Caulker would rule areas south of the Cockboro Creek.

Although Canreba ruled peacefully after the war, there remained a lot of animosity between his children and Thomas Stephen's children, as well as between their respective subjects. Always preparing for war, Canreba continued to build his army and gave the area now called Rotifunk to a Loko chief, Sorie Kessebe and his people, so that they could be nearby incase he needed their warrior services. In later years, this move created a problem when the missionaries were given the same area to build their mission.

3. **1857-1864 Thomas Theophilus Caulker**—succeeded his brother James Canreba. He was educated at the school on Plantain Island which was being run by his cousin Thomas Stephen's family. In spite of his education, he was considered a weak ruler, and had trouble maintaining order among his section chiefs. He tried to bring in Mende war boys to fight against the section chiefs, but they had also hired war boys to fight against their chief. With the threat of war, a Poro signal was placed on the Timber, halting the production. He was eventually able to get naval assistance from the Colony, to assert his power, but when the navy left, Pa Keni, the section chief in Ribbi, declared his section independent of the Bompeh chiefdom. This was an economic blow to the chiefdom, as Ribbi was the site of the income producing timber factories. This separation caused an inevitable economic downturn, and probably caused the slow disintegration of the Bompeh chifdom. By the time Thomas Theophilus died in 1864, Ribbi was completely independent.

4. **1865-1901 Richard Canreba Caulker**—son of Canreba succeeded his uncle Theophilus. He was the first Caulker chief to be educated in the Colony. With a scholarship from the colonial government he attended the CMS Grammar School (the boys school which opened in 1846 in Freetown). Like his uncle, Richard inherited and continued the feud with the Plantain/Shenge Caulkers which his father Canreba had started. He joined the Poro society in order to get help to continue the fight.

    Although he often compared himself to the kings of the Bible and of English history, few people gave him the respect he thought he should have had as their chief. But inspite of his Grammar School education and his Poro membership, Richard was still unable to maintain control over his chiefdom.

    On December 1881, he was one of the signatories of the revived 1825 Turner Treaty, which brought the Caulker Chiefdoms under British rule. The Caulkers formally acknowledged the treaty and dispelled any doubts about their legal rights to levy customs tariffs in their country. The stipend which they had received in the beginning, was increased from £70.00 sterling to £100.00

In 1883, the Yoni were looking for a port on the Ribbi or Bompeh rivers, where they could trade with the colony traders. They entered Ribbi in 1884 and plundered the timber factories. They also invaded Bompeh. But this area which had been ceded under the Turner Treaty, was now a British territory and Governor (Pinkett) believed that it was to be treated as such. So he sent police from the colony to help fight against the Yoni. His men assisted the old Kono chief, Sorie Kesebe, who had been given land around the Rotifunk area by James Canreba. This Rotifunk area was well fortified with Kesebe's own Loko men and about 200 Fulas. There was a strong suspiscion that Richard was secretly supporting the Yoni against Sorie Kesebe during this crisis, but he denied the charge and it seems nothing was made of it.

Richard assisted his cousin William Caulker of Mambo, during the latter's fight with chief Thomas Neale-Caulker of Plantain/Shenge. In 1888, at the end of that quarrel, Richard and William were imprisoned in Freetown. After William's trial and execution, Richard was exiled to the Gambia, where he was told "to go and meditate on the tarnished glories of the House of Caulker". He was reinstated in 1894, at the height of the debate about the payment of hut taxes. At first he forbade his people to pay the tax but for some reason, he changed his mind and started collecting the tax. Governor Cardew believed that Richard was associated with another chief, Bai Kompa in a scheme. So he had Richard jailed in Kwelu. While he was there, Richard admitted that although he had paid £10.00 sterling in taxes, he had sent £70.00 to Koinadugu, where the government could not find it. Richard Canreba Caulker died in jail in Freetown in 1901.

5. **1899-1903-James Canreba Caulker**—succeeded his father Richard Canreba Caulker but ruled for 4 years. His children included Charles, Peter, Albert and James. His son Peter was the father of Mary (who later became Mrs. Max Bailor) and his son Albert later became chief.

6. **1904-1907-John Canreba Caulker**—succeeded his brother James Canreba, but ruled for only 3 years.

7. **1907-1921—Thomas Canreba Caulker**—succeeded his brother John. At first he was hesitant to accept the Staff, because, he realized that the two chiefs before him had ruled for only 4 years each and he was himself passed middle age. He constulted Spiritualists as far away as the Gambia and was told that the reason his predecessors ruled for such a short time, was because Richard, their father had not been buried in family cemetery. He had been buried in Freetown after he died in jail. Richard's body was eventually exhumed and brought to the family cemetery, and Thomas agreed to take the Staff. He ruled for 14 years.

Thomas Canreba Caulker He was the father of Mabel Caulker, one of the first students enrolled at the Harford School for girls. She later became the mother of the Karefa-Smart family.

The article below, told by his grandson, the late Dr. John Karefa-Smart, describes life with the chief.

> *"My mother's father, Thomas Canray Bah Caulker was paramount Chief of the Bompeh Chiefdom when I was born in Rotifunk, a town named by Temne speaking Lokko warriors. The town was built near the source of the Bompeh River which flows west to the Yawri Bay.*
>
> *After the Hut Tax War, during which five missionaries were killed and their building destroyed, new missionaries from America rebuilt the Church which they named 'The Martyrs Memorial Church', as well as an elementary school and a dispensary. My grandfather enrolled his favorite daughter Mabel as a student in the new school. Mabel was the daughter of his Fula wife Yebu, who was a princess of the Bunuka Clan. When The Harford School for Girls was built in Moyamba, my mother was one of the first students transferred to the new school. After completing the Harford school my mother married James Alfred Karefa-Smart, the young pastor of the Martyr's Memorial Church. As a wedding gift, grandpa built a house for his daughter opposite the Mission compound. We heard the story of how, on mother's wedding day, Grandpa had country cloths spread all the way from his compound across the Bompeh River bridge to the church, so that his daughter would not have to walk to her wedding on bare ground.*

> Before starting school at the age of six, I remember spending many days visiting grandpa Caulker when he was not away at Kassipoto, his hometown down river. When I was eight years old, he arranged that my older brother Thomas and I be initiated into the Poro society. On "coming out day", there was a grand celebration at Kassipoto. Obai and I dressed in new gowns and were seated in places of honor besides Grandpa, We were given our new Poro names.
>
> Soon after we became Poro members, Grandpa Caulker died from internal injuries he sustained when one of his hammock carriers stumbled and grandpa was thrown to the ground. On the way to the funeral in Bompeh, the new ancestral burial place of the Bompeh Caulker chiefs, my brother and I traveled in a canoe with one of our maternal uncles. This uncle told us that, as favorite grand children, we would have the honor of accompanying grandpa on his trip to the next world.
>
> When the drumming and dancing which had gone on during the funeral came to an end, I realized grandpa would no longer be with us. His death became real.

Note that today, the Bompeh chiefs who carried the name Canreba, are now referred to as **Kainba**. They are the descendants of Canreba Caulker.

6. **1921-1954—Albert G. Caulker**—Chief A.G. Caulker or Gbosowah (as he was commonly known) was the son of James Canreba and grandson of Theophillus. At the time of his succession, Fosoma Koroma, was allowed to contest for the Bompeh chieftaincy, but A.G. Caulker defeated him. He was the first chief from the protectorate to sit on the Executive Council of Sierra Leone. He had 11 wives and many children. Among his children were Priscilla (Mrs Clay), Rachel (Mrs.Caulker), Arthur, Nancy and Nora (Mrs. Yanni).
7. **1954-1983—William I. Caulker**—this grandson of James Canreba succeeded his cousin the late A.G Caulker. He was chief when, in 1961, Sierra Leone was granted independence by the British, under the Sierra Leone People's Party (SLPP). On April 26th 1968, after much political unrest, with coups and counter coups, Mr. Siaka Stevens was sworn in as Prime Minister, heading the All People's Congress

(APC). Being a staunch SLPP member, he was part of the opposition, as well as being a Paramount Chief—an unenviable position to be in at the time, because during the rule of the All Peoples Congress (APC party), attempts were made to install chiefs who were in the party's favor and certainly not members of the opposition. William was allegedly beaten up in 1983 by members of the APC, and died from his wounds. He was succeeded by his son Charles.

8. **1984-present. Charles Caulker**—This son of William, is also a member of parliament. Charles participated on the committee which set policy for the succession of Paramount chiefs, in order to correct the confusion which had been created in the process of crowning legitimate paramount chiefs from legitimate ruling houses.

Today, Government Policy states that: ***One can only be a chief, if the House for which a candidate is standing, was established before the Independence of Sierra Leone in 1961.***(P.C. Charles Caulker of Bompeh)

THE KAGBORO CHIEFDOM CAULKER CHIEFS.

THE PLANTAIN/SHENGE CAULKERS

1. **1810-1831 George Stephen Caulker I (Ba Charch)**—On his return from school in England, George had asked his uncle, chief Thomas Kon Tham if he could rule part of the 'Old Kagbor' chiefdom. The chief agreed, and with the help of his brother Thomas Stephen, the Plantain/Shenge Chiefdom was established.

   George Stephen had three sons, Stephen George, Charles George and Thomas George (Kugba). The first two of his sons died, leaving Thomas Kugba as the sole survivor. When George Stephen I died in 1831, Thomas was too young to become chief. So his uncle Thomas Stephen was made Regent Chief, ostensibly to rule until Thomas came of age.

2. **1831-1871—Thomas Stephen Caulker (Ba Tham)**. Although Thomas Stephen began his rule as the Regent Chief, he continued to rule even after Thomas Kugba became old enough to rule. He did not give up

the chiefdom to Thomas Kugba because he felt he was better suited to be chief because he had more experience as a ruler, since he had worked with George Stephen I while the Plantain/Shenge chiefdom was being established. Clearly his nephew Thomas resented him for that, and joined his uncle Canreba in retaliation. After the war, a treaty was signed which specified that 'Canreba would rule the area north of the Cockboro Creek and Thomas Stephen would rule the area south of the Cockboro Creek. At their death the chiefdom would be reunited under a descendant of George Stephen I.' That never happened.

During his rule, Thomas Stephen founded the town of Shenge in 1840 and signed a treaty with the Brithish to annex the Banana Islands to the Colony. The United Brethren missionaries arrived in 1855, but although he agreed to give them 100 acres of land to do their work, he was very hostile towards them. He refused to attend their church meetings and forbade his people to attend as well. When his daughter Lucy joined the church he became very angry and sent her off to be married to a trader on York Island. It was not until a black missionary, Joseph Gomer and his wife Mary, arrived in 1871 that Thomas agreed to join their church. Thomas died later that year, leaving behind 23 children.

By the time Thomas Stephen died, Thomas Kugba had died and his son William Thomas George Caulker was off trading in the Gallinas and was not present for the selection of a new chief. Hence, Thomas Stephen was succeeded by his son George Stephen II.

3. **1871-1881—George Stephen II**—This son of Thomas Stephen had worked as an interpreter to the missionaries at Shenge. He was the first to translate the Bible into the Sherbro language, but it was never published. During his reign he quarreled with his cousin John Caulker who was then the speaker of the chiefdom. John brought Mende war boys to attack his cousin. John had a large force from Gbanya, and he and his men plundered and destroyed the Bagru country. This war lasted until November 1875, when a Commandant, Darrell Davis, who had been appointed by the Colonial Government in 1874, came to the chief's aid with a few policemen and men who had been supplied by the Bagru chief. By the end of that war, Davis who had been badly wounded, was sent back to England.

Meanwhile, with support from the chief, Rev. Gomer continued to work on his mission. He built a stone chapel and a mission house for the U.B.C. in Shenge. He also opened mission stations nearby. Through Gomer and the Caulkers, the UBC entrenched itself in Sherbro land in a way no other mission body had done before.

George II died during a trip to Freetown in 1881. The governor, had invited him to Freetown, in an attempt to broker a peace agreement, between the himself and William of Mambo. But George was ill when he arrived in Freetown, and had to have emergency surgery. He died during the procedure and was taken to Tasso for burial. Governor Havelock, ignoring the traditional process for crowning a chief, decided that George's half brother Thomas Neale-Caulker, who had accompanied him to Freetown, would be the Regent Chief.

4. **1881-1898—Thomas Neale-Caulker**—Thomas Neale-Caulker's ascent to the throne created a lot of unrest in the chiefdom. But this was soon quelled and Thomas remained chief. Peace was brokered between himself and William, but although they were outwardly reconciled, they remained bitter enemies. Thomas frequently sent reports or complaints about William to the Colonial Government.

   During his rule, Thomas Neale-Caulker was hated by many of his chiefs. He was considered to be oppressive and harsh and many of his subjects still thought of him as a usurper of the throne. As far as they were concerned, his cousin William was the one who had been wronged. Thomas was however, loyal to the government which he knew had appointed him as chief, and had upheld his chieftaincy. So when the issue of paying a Hut Tax came up, although his half sister Lucy (the first UBC convert) told him to refuse to pay the tax, he said nothing and went along with the edict. With help from the government, the taxes were collected under brutal conditions. Inevitably, war broke out in the Protectorate. During the Hut Tax War as it was called, Thomas Neale-Caulker was assassinated.

5. **1898-1909—Sophia Neale-Caulker (Yemi Bei—Madam Chief)**. Because the assassinated chief had been loyal to the British government, his wife was given the staff of office as Paramount Chief of the Plantain/Shenge Chiefdom. Sophia Neale-Caulker, was the grand daughter of George Stephen I (Ba Charch) and wife of Thomas Stephen's son.

During her rule, the population of Shenge increased to 200, but cannibalism became rampant along the Kagboro coast. No one felt safe and people were afraid to leave their homes or even sleep at home. There were those who believed, although they could not verify it, that there was political backing for this situation. These rumors of cannibalism were embarrassing to the chief, and led to her ultimate deposition.

Uniting the Plantain/Shenge chiefdom with the Kagboro District

During Madam Neale-Caulker's reign, the question of uniting the Kagboro district with the Shenge/Plantain chiefdom arose. A woman by the name of Mammy Negbo, claimed that there were two separate rights of chieftaincy in the Shenge District, under the Blue Book (C1402 of 1856)—the rights of the Cumba-Caulker House and those of the Sosant Dick House. There had been a long standing controversy between the two ruling houses in both districts, since the Kagboro district was separate and independent from the Plantain/Shenge Chiefdom. By 1908, the people in Kagboro revolted against the Shenge chief and sent several letters and petitions from the District to the Colonial Government. A section chief, Sei Lebbi, along with other section chiefs from the district asked to be separated from Shenge.

On December 19th a meeting was held. Among those present was the Governor, Captain Edward Fairlough, (who had succeeded Governor Cardew). The agenda for that meeting, included discussions on how the district was being ruled by Madam Sophia and her section chiefs. Their Mode of conducting local court, and Mode of Trading were also questioned. *(Tower)*. Chief Sophia Neal Caulker was generally described as, a very weak ruler, whose chiefdom was virtually run by the Domingo family.

On December 22nd 1908, the governor declared that Kagboro District would be placed under the Paramount Chief of Plantain/Shenge. He also ruled that Paramount chief, Madam Sophia Neale-Caulker was too old to be chief and should retire. (Records showed that she was morbidly obese, weighing 400 lbs. and could barely move). The ruling also stated that, at the time of her retirement, all her officers would be relieved of their power, and all of the section chiefs would be responsible for their own sections until another paramount chief could be crowned.

To prevent coercion of the natives as they selected a new chief, the governor also granted pardon to all Poro members whose activities had been banned due to their part in the Hut Tax War. (*Records in the archives at Fourah Bay college*)

That year, the District of Kagboro was combined with the Plantain/Shenge chiefdom, and the chiefdom became the Kagboro Chiefdom. (One can imagine that by now the Cumba-Caulker House was probably in a state of chaos, trying to hastily decide who would stand as chief.)

6. **1909-1911—Sei Lebbi**—On February 8th 1909, Sei Lebbi of the Sosant Dick House of Mocobo was chosen as the first Paramount Chief of Kagboro Chiefdom. Lebbi promptly move the chiefdom headquarters to Mocobo (the chiefdom seat of that ruling house.) Shenge was left in ruins. The Caulkers who were quite dissatisfied with this move mounted a protest. This took over a decade to settle. In the meantime, two years after he became chief, Lebbi was replaced by Gbana Bome, the former steward and betrayer of Chief Thomas Neale-Caulker.

7. **1917-1917(6 months)—Gbana Bome**—It seems to have taken several years of chaos before another leader was chosen. When a chief was finally chosen, it was the man who had betrayed his chief during the Hut Tax war,—an act which resulted in the chief's assanination. Gbana Bome ruled for 6 months, from his headquarters in Pujehun. For those who firmly believe that the Caulker Ancestors do take their revenge if a Caulker has been wronged, reports came stating that before his death that same year, Gbana Bome became deaf, dumb and blind, they felt that the Caulkers had been avenged.

8. **1917-1919—Kwe Boka—.**—Kwe Boka succeeded Gbana Bome, and ruled for only two years. By that time, the Caulkers had finally reorganized themselves and in 1919, they were able to win back the staff.

9. **1919-1933—Samuel Africanus Caulker**—Grandson of Thomas Stephen Caulker, **w**as considered one of the most dynamic rulers in Kagboro Chiefdom. But shortly after he became chief, the specter

of cannibalism began to rear its ugly head again. People were threatened with images of baboons and leopards on land, and alligators and something called 'kungkbe' in the rivers. It seemed that the aim of the perpetrators was to demoralize the people and to blame the chief with the hope of bringing an early end to his rule. This was clearly an attempt to vilify the Caulker House. In order to wipe out this menace and prove his innocence, the chief, with the permission of the District Officers and chiefdom authorities, arranged to use native medicine and charms to put a curse on whoever was doing this. It worked! For a few months, the medicine which had been used, smelled out the wrongdoers and those who had engaged in such malpractices. Within a year some of the section chiefs and several leading influential people in the chiefdom had died and there was peace in the land.

His tenure in office restored the glory of the Caulkers which had been tainted by the removal of the chieftaincy to Mocobo for almost a decade. Shenge was rebuilt. The chief's compound and the Court Barrie which looked so graceful and dignified, were built in 1920 under the leadership of George Caulker of Mambo.

In order to increase enrollment in the Rufus Clark and Wife School which had also been renovated, two boys were selected from each of the seventeen sections of the chiefdom and placed in boarding school.

In February 1932, the first motor vehicle—a lorry owned by a Syrian trader, Simon Bamin of Moyamba, arrived in Shenge. It was a memorable day for the residents of villages along the way, for they had never seem a motor vehicle. Thus began a twice weekly routine, for the lorries which arrived on Mondays and Fridays, spent the night, then loaded up for the return trip. Shenge was now able to send fish and other items for sale in Moyamba. Chief Sam Caulker died in 1933.

10. **1933-1954—Rev. Alphonso Theophilus (A.T.) Caulker Gbabiyor I**—an ordained minister in the Evangelical United Brethren Church. (EUB), succeeded Chief Sam Caulker.

In 1936 the Native Administration (the local government) was introduced in Kagboro and In 1942, the first chiefdom office was built.

In 1950, members of a secret society called 'Ojeh' made up of Temne men who were foreign to the area, crossed over from Ribbi Chiefdom to Kagboro. They joined the Temne fishermen in a near by village called Kartha and created a disturbance, as they tried to introduce their society by force. They threatened the lives of the Sherbro people, beat them up, looted their farms and threatened to kill the chiefdom Speaker, Mr. Moses Barrow. Moses escaped in the middle of the night, taking with him a letter from the chief to the District Officer. The letter described the situation in the chiefdom. The District Officer responded immediately and sent several policemen to Kartha. They rounded up the invaders and took them to Moyamba, where they were tried and imprisoned. But this did not solve the problem. The crisis continued and government sent a Temne Chief—paramount Chief Alikalimodu of Port Lokko, to investigate the disturbance. Eventually Ojeh was banned in Kagboro Chiefdom and did not rear its head in the chiefdom again until the 1970's when it was reintroduced by politicians. The chief allowed the Temne residents to be made Tribal Counselors in the chiefdom, probably as a way to keep the peace.

On October 13th 1954, rules of the Native Courts and the Native Appeals Court were written by the Attorney General, Mr. S.A. Benka-Coker. These rules read:

1. **Any native dissatisfied with the decision of the Native Court, may appeal to the Native Appeals Court, which is headed by the District Commissioner.**
2. **Every appeal will be entered within one calendar year, either orally or by petition. Fees will be credited to the revenue of the chiefdom.** *(Sierra Leone Archives)*

After the death of Chief A.T. Caulker in 1954, the two ruling houses—Ya-Cumba and Sosant-Dick, once again vied for the chieftaincy. The contest was a very keen one and all the contestants were notable and influential. Ballot boxes were used for the first time but once again the Caulkers were in disarray. The Cumba-Caulker house was split. Now there were three houses vying for the

Chieftaincy—The Cumba-Caulker House, 'The Caulker House' and Sosant-Dick house. One could ask, why there were two Caulker houses contesting, when both were of the same stock? There does not seem to be an answer. Needless to say, Gbono Dick, of the Sosant-Dick House in Mocobo won the election. There is much to be said about the adage *"United we stand, Divided we fall".* Which is what happened in this case.

11. **1955-1960—Gbono Dick**—During his rule, there were strikes all over the country against local tax increases. In 1956, riots ensued all over the country, and property was destroyed. Several chiefdoms, including Kagboro were affected.

    That same year, a health center was built in Shenge.

    In 1958, Ghanaian fishermen arrived and settled in Shenge, creating a dispute between resident Temne fishermen and the Ghanaians, who were using a method of fishing which was foreign to the Temnes. This created more unrest.

    It is said that during his short rule, Chief Gbono Dick had recurrent dreams of the Caulker Ancestors, which caused him to become insane. He died in 1960 after a prolonged illness. By this time the Caulkers once again seemed to have regrouped, and won the ensuing elections.

12. **1961-1999—Honoria Bailor-Caulker**—grand daughter of Madam Sophia Neale-Caulker, was crowned. That year (1961) Sierra Leone gained its independence from the British Crown and in 1971 became a Republic. As Teacher Tower puts it, *"Sierra Leone became a country of "Politricks" in the districts, the chiefdoms and towns, in the houses and streets and even in families. Everyone became an enemy and a suspected villain."* This system of "politricks" was deeply rooted in Kagboro Chiefdom, and brought multiple disputes and enquiries between the Paramount Chief and the Chiefdom Speaker, the tribal councilors and the Temne of Plantain Island.

    In 1962, most of the Ghanaian fishermen moved from Shenge, but there seemed to be an insoluble cold war between the Temnes and those Ghanaians who had chosen to stay behind, and between the Members of Parliament and the Paramount Chief. Each had strong political backing, and 'Politricks' seemed to be the order of the day.

In 1967, the Howard Memorial School was built by the International Development Agency (I.D.A) and a secondary school program, sponsored by the World Bank, was established.

The Fisheries Department was also established in Shenge.

Several people from Kagboro Chiefdom, including the Paramount Chief herself, became members of parliament. The chief represented the district chiefs, and the other parliamentarian representatives from Kagboro, including Mr, Valecius B. Caulker, grandson of Sophia Neale-Caulker, Mr. Kelfala, Mr. A.F.Williams and Mr. Harry T.T.Williams, all represented the constituency.

In the late 1970's, Shenge was once again destroyed and several historic buildings, including Madam Bailor-Caulker's compound. (She had to build her own compound, since the old chief's compound, was now owned by the descendants of Chief A.T. Caulker.)

During the Rebel War of 1990-2001, the chief was forced into hiding in the bush, but was later able to flee to the United States, where she died in 1999.

Her death created another round of complete chaos within the Caulker family. There was no semblance of unity. In a fashion similar to the events which followed the death of Chief A.T.Caulker, family members from the same ruling house—the Cumba-Caulker house, contested against each other. Brothers—John and Tennyson Caulker, initially contested against their sister Doris Lenga-Kroma. *(All of them were children of A.T.Caulker.* Their nephew Thomas Caulker also contested against his uncles and aunt. The elders were reluctant to commit to one candidate, (saying they did not want to insult the other candidates who were relatives). There was no guidance to be had from them.

John and Tennyson eventually backed down in favor of their sister, leaving Thomas to run against his aunt Doris. Into this mix came someone, Sigismund 'Old Man' Caulker, who was unfamiliar to the Ya-Cumba Caulkers, claimed he was from Tisana in the north of the chiefdom No one was quite sure whether he represented the Sosant-Dick House, and no one could make his connection with the Cumba-Caulkers, although he claimed to have been raised in P.C.

Samuel Caulker's household. Sigismund entered the contest, and was backed by polititians such as Mr. Harry T.T. Williams.

Meanwhile, Ojeh once again raised its head.! There were those in the chiefdom who strongly felt that they did not want a female chief because they had been disillusioned and disappointed by the last female chief. In fear for their lives, after being forced by Ojeh leadership to take an oath in the bush, which said that they would not vote for a woman, some of the voters were willing to swing their votes toward Aunty Doris's opponents. Still others simply gave their votes to the highest bidder or to the one who promised better things to come—a bag of rice went a long way. For the first time in this writer's memory, many Caulkers in the Diaspora were able to express their opinions on the matter, and some took sides. Once again the Caulker family was disunited and in a state of chaos.

On election day ballots were cast and in the end Sigismund won the election and was crowned chief of Kagboro chiefdom and Thomas Caulker was made his chiefdom speaker.

13. **2003-2008—Sigismund 'Old Man' Caulker**—During his rule, there was not much accomplished within the chiefdom. Kagboro chiefdom deteriorated even further. But the women had made a strong showing during the election, and they were not done!!!

Determined that the family would not lose its heritage, Doris lenga—Kroma (Aunty Doris) made a legal protest, and in 2004, mounted a petition claiming irregularities in the process of naming and crowning Sigismund Caulker as chief of Kagboro.

The case was heard in the Law Courts in Freetown, and on Friday April 4th 2009, after five long years in court, Doris's bid finally paid off and a decision was made. Chief Sigismund Old Man Caulker was asked to step down immediately, and according to the Chieftaincy Act of 2009, the staff was retrieved and a Regent chief was installed. Plans were made for new elections to be held after the revision of the Councillors' list.

The Caulker family had finally began to work together as a unit. Elections were conducted on December 29th 2009 and this time, with the family solidly behind her, Doris Lenga-Kroma won the election.

14. **2010-present—P.C. Rev. Doris Lenga-Caulker Gbabiyor II**—is the daughter of P.C. A.T. Caulker. Like her father before her, she is an ordained minister in the United Methodist church.

The following is the description of her inauguration in her own words.

> "Through God's intervention, the Caulker House has regained the Kagboro Chieftaincy Staff, which is our Heritage.
>
> Based on the petition mounted by the Caulkers led by me, which stated that 'Sigismund Oldman Caulker did not have a right to the Caulker Chieftaincy Staff', the High Court of Sierra Leone gave its verdict on April 4th 2009 in favor of the Caulkers.
>
> On December 29 2009, elections were conducted and the Caulkers won through their flag bearer Rev. Doris Lenga-Kroma nee Caulker. It was a day of joy for both young and old of the family, friends, supporters and chiefdom people.
>
> Wednesday April 7th 2010 was a day to be remembered by the Kagboro people. That was the day His Excellency the President of Sierra Leone, Dr. Ernest Bai Koroma officially gave the staff of office to the new paramount chiefs. I was flanked by my people in 'Fenteh' gowns and shirts as I went to in to the ceremony to receive the long awaited Staff.
>
> On Thurday April 8th 2010, I was driven to Shenge the capital of Kagbor and was greeted by dancers as we drove passed the towns and villages of the chiefdom. When we entered Shenge Town, the throngs of people with palms and green branches could not be contained. There was merriment and dancing throughout the night. I shed tears of joy and in my heart, humbly thanked God for the honor which was being given to me.
>
> On Friday April 9th I joined the Muslims in their Friday Muslim prayers, after which the whole "Jahma" (the group of worshippers) walked me home, praising Allah for their new chief. Again, I privately thanked God for religious tolerance.
>
> Saturday April 10th was another day of rejoicing. This was the day the Paramount Chief was officially presented to her people who, through their Section Chiefs, pledged their loyalty to their Paramount

Chief. Symbolic royalties such as the soil, palmoil, rice, fish, water and a goat, were presented to me as the custodian of the chiefdom. This was indeed a solemn act. Following this ceremony, traditional dancers danced through the rest of the day and night.

Sunday Aprill 11th, was the climax of the celebration. It was the day for the Thanksgiving service which was held at the Gomer Memorial United Methodist Church. The UMC conference was represented by the Rev. Moses Conteh and the clerical staff of the UMC office. Rev. David H. Caulker, who represented Bishop John K. Yambaso, (the UMC bishop) gave the message with the theme, 'A joyful new beginning'. After making pledges to God and the congregation, we received Communion. This ended the journey which began on December 9th 2002.

I have learned a few lessons from my journey to the chieftaincy, which I would like to share:

It pays to stand for the truth, no matter how long it may take to show up. In the end, it will surely yield its fruits of truth.

In order to succeed, we, as a family, must stand together in unity. As the saying goes, "United we stand, divided we fall."

Above all, "when a man's ways are pleasing to the Lord, he makes even his enemies live in peace with him. (Proverbs 16:7)

A final message to you all: "Come let us rebuild the walls of Kagboro and we will no longer be in disgrace." (Nehemiah 2:17)

I thank you all for the support which you have given in a number of ways. Please continue the support, so Kagboro can move forward."

PEACE

Paramount Chief Doris Lenga Gbabiyor Caulker II

Appendix II

A Walking Tour Around the Old Town of Shenge

The year is about **1940**. We have arrived by Lorry, since there are no cars or vans which come down to this area. Our lorry drops us off at the entrance to the town. We enter Shenge from the Sembehun road (so called, because Sembehun is that last Lorry stop before Shenge). As we walk down the road, on the right, we stop for a brief visit at the home of **Orlando Caulker**. Uncle Orlando is the son of **Jasper Caulker**, AKA Pa Jasper.

When we leave Uncle Orlando, we come to the junction where the road branches. The road to the right goes to Dibiya, where **Zilpa Caulker (Mama Kai Thi)** lives. She is married to Pa Dillet. Their daughter Nora Dillet (Mi Chauni) is married to Gabriel Deen of Mambo House. The Deens are the parents of **Salimatu Deen-Tonkara and Marie Deen.**

On the side of the Dibiya road is a dense forest known as the Mambo Bundu Bush. Next to this, is the Coconut Plantation which is said to have been planted by **Griffith Caulker**. At this junction, we turn left and head towards the Bolahun Road which will take us to the chief's compound.

As we continue on our way, the first home we come to on the left, belongs to the Neale family. **Dan and Tommy**, were known as **The Neale brothers**. Dan was the father of the late **Lois Karimu and the late Dwight Neale**. Tommy married Lucian Caulker and they had five daughters, **Agnes, Angela, Laura, Hortense and Sophia**.

Futher down the road, is the home of **Rev. Michael M. Caulker (Uncle M.M.)**, who is the father of **Grace, Alvalin and Franklyn**, a popular guitarist often heard on the radio.

Across the road from Uncle M.M. is the home of **Priscilla Blaize-Caulker** mother of **the late Paramount Chief Honoria Bailor Caulker** and **the late Clive Remie**.

Continuing our journey, we go passed the road which leads to Mobetti, the home of **Rose Caulker-Cole**. At the fork, we turn left passed the clinic which is at the junction. Further down this road is the home of Pa Griffith, famous for his Coconu Plantation mentioned above. The memorable landmark at this junction is the large peach mango tree.

Across the road from the clinic is the area called San Domingo, or New Home. This is the home of **Frances Caulker-Domingo**, wife of **George Domingo, (former Chiefdom Speaker during the reign of Chief Sophia Neale-Caulker and famous for his Caulker-Manuscripts)**.

Further down the Bolahun road, in the opposite direction from our destination, is the home of the **Barlays (a family closely linked to the Caulkers, by marriage)** and the home of the **Manley family**. If we go further down, we come to Bonguma Cemetery also known as 'The other cemetery' where non-Caulkers are buried.

Back on the main road we go passed **Old Pa Jasper Caulker's** house. Pa Jasper was the son of **P.C. Chief Samuel Caulker** who preceded **P.C. Chief A.T.Caulker**. Next to Pa Jasper, is the **Mosque** which is followed by the home of **the Myers family. Teacher Myers, his wife Flora, (daughter of Rev. S.B. Caulker) and their children Sunbeam, Elsiemae, Laurel, Laurence, Stephen and Albert (Chico)**. When the family moved, the house was given to the chief's eldest daughter, **Gladys Caulker-Lefevre**, mother of **Annie Bangura, the late Dwight Lefevre and Lucy Sumner**. Next door to Aunty Gladys is the pharmacy which was run by **Uncle Moss Caulker** and across the way is a store run by **Mama Iye**, the widow of Chief Sam Caulker.

As we continue our journey, we must stop at the home of **Aunty Lucia Stevens**, mother of **Amy Challe**. Aunty Amy's children are **Helen, the late Albert, the late Charles and Edna Challe**. Across the way from aunty Lucia's is the parsonage, the homes of the Andersons and the Browns. But we must now head to the original chief's compound.

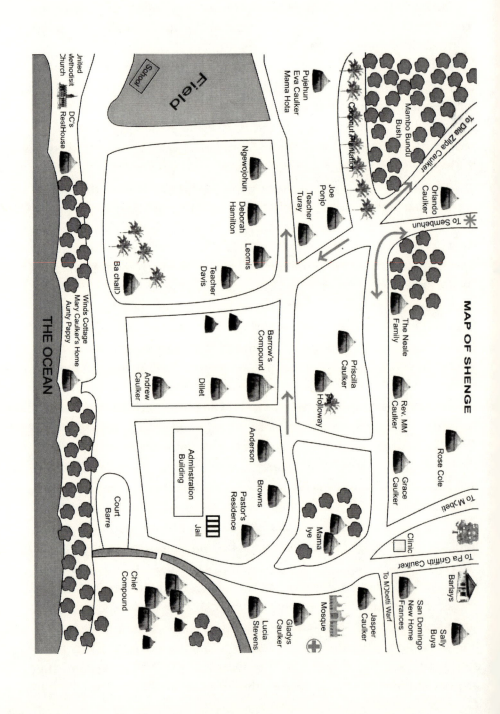

The chief's compound was built by **George Caulker of Mambo**, for chief Sam Caulker. It was planned and built primarily for security. The outer wall which surrounds the compound on three sides (the fourth side is the ocean), was built with living quarters for the guards. Inside the compound is the main house, along with several smaller buildings. In the middle of the compound, several feet from the main house, is a large mango tree with a bench which faces the sea. To the right of the main building is the court Barre where the chief sits to hear chiefdom matters. Across the way is the administration building, which houses the District Commissioner's offices. The town jail is next door.

As we walk passed the barre, we are now on the road which runs along the ocean. Ahead on the left facing the ocean, not far from the barre, is the area which was once the home of **Mary Caulker-French (AKA Aunty Pappy), Daughter of William Caulker of Mambo. Her siblings were Rev. S.B.Caulker, Agnes Caulker-Campbell, Benson and Nat Caulker.** Nat, like many other Caulkers and Sierra Leoneans, went to Nigeria to work in the Civil Service and Rev. S.B.Caulker went to Bonthe. Mary herself the mother of Randolph French, was the midwife of Shenge and was known as a very powerful lady.

Across the road from Aunty Pappy's is the home of **Andrew Caulker**, and up the street from him on the corner, is the Barrow Compound. **Pa Barrow** was the chiefdom speaker.

Of interest is the fact that the Barrows, Campbells, Dillets and Domingos, are said to be descended from a group of men called the West Indian Frontiersmen, who had come to work for the colony of Sierra Leone. It seems that they all married Caulker women!.

We continue walking along this ocean road and soon come to Ba Challor—which means "Under the Palm" because it is located under some palm trees. This is the home of **Sarah Caulker-Woolsy.** Sarah had a daughter **Miriam Lewis,** by **Sir Samuel Lewis,** the first Sierra Leonean Chief Justice in 1882, the first mayor of the colony in 1895 and the first African to be knighted in 1896. Sarah also had a son, **Mr. G.D.Caulker, who became the father of Andrew, Dulcie and Melvin. Andrew became the father of Prince, Dwight, Enid, the late Sym, and Lawrence.**

In that same block are the homes of Teacher Davis, and **Deborah Caulker-Hamilton.**

Further down the road is the District Commissioner's rest house. Not too far away is the Gomer Memorial United Bretheren Church (UBC now United Methodist Church UMC), with its cemetery, where many Caulkers are buried.

Now we turn right passed the school with its large football field and further up that road we com to Pujehun, home of **Eva Caulker (Mamo Hota), mother of Doyle, Marion, Millicent and Irene.** After we bid her goodbye, we set off down the road, passed the homes of Teacher Turay and Joe Ponjo on our way back towards the Sembehun road, to catch our lorry back to freetown.

The information for this 'tour' was given by ***Elsie Mae Kallon, Laurel Turay*** *and* ***Mildred Caulker****, all of whom grew up in Shenge. Their invaluable information has enabled me to create this 'tour' of Shenge.*

ICB.

Appendix III

The Treaties

Taken from **'The Handbook of Sierra Leone'** by T.N. Goddard.

Treaty # 7, which was signed on July 21st 1820, with Governor MacCarthy, A Pa London of Koya, ceded the Banana islands to the Government in his own name on behalf of Thomas Kon Tham Caulker, for an annual payment of 100 bars to himself and his successors, and 50 bars to Kon Tham and his successors.

Treaty # 8—October 20th 1820,—the Banana Island was ceded again, this time by Thomas Kon Tham Caulker and George Stephen Caulker, in return for an annual payment to them and their successor of 250 bars, payable in Spanish dollars, at the rate of one dollar to one bar. . . . Excerpts from the Treaty say, *"That Thomas Caulker and George Stephen Caulker for and on the part and behalf of themselves and their successors, . . . have this day ceded, transferred and given to his said Honour Acting Governor Grant . . . the full, entire, free and unlimited possesion and sovereignty of the said islands of Bananas and lands in their immediate vicinity . . . His said Honor the Acting Governor . . . agrees to pay yearly and every year to Thomas Caulker and George Stephen Caulker collectively and their successors, the sum of 250 bars . . . His said Honour the Acting Governor . . . guarantees to Thomas Caulker and George Stephen Caulker . . . free possession of the lands, houses or property of whatever kind which they do now or may possess on the said islands . . . It is* further agreed that the payment of the afore said rent or custom shal l become due payable on the 1st day of October each year and shall be paid in Spanish dollars at the rate of one dollar to one bar, thence forth and forever . . . Failure of the regular payment above agreed upon the present treaty shall be considered null and void." (Sierra Leone Archives, Fourah Bay College)

Treaty #12—September 24th 1825—The Turner Treaty—The Caulkers representing the Ya Kumba house, Banka of Yoni, King of Sherbro and their section chiefs, signed a treaty with Governor Charles Turner, giving up sovereignty between the Kamaranka and Kamalay (between Sherbro island and the Gallinas) and became British subjects.

Excerpts from the Treaty read—" *Whereas a cruel and destructive war has for several years raged between certain tribes of the Kusso nation and the inhabitants of countries bordering on the Sherbro Bulloms, which countries the said tribes of the Kussos have conquered and destroyed, and the defenceless inhabitants of which they have cruelly murdered or sold into slavery: and whereas the said Kusso tribes have commenced hostilities against the Sherbro Bulloms and have overrun and depopulated part of the territories belonging to the said Bankah, King of Sherbro and Ya Comba, Queen of Ya Comba . . . That they have of their own free will and accord stepped forward and thrown themselves and their countries upon the protection of his Excellency the Governor General of Sierra Leone and the British Government, as the surest means of saving themselves and subjects from the destruction threatened by their cruel and implacable enemies: and whereas in the progress of the said war violent outrages have been commited by parties to the said war, upon the property and persons of British subjects engaged in lawful trade and commerce, plundering the one, seizing and selling into slavery the others . . . And whereas his Excellency the Governor General of Sierra Leone, feeling no less apprehension for the peace and security of his Britannic Majesty's territories, the war having already approached the frontiers of the colony of Sierra Leone, than indignation at the insults offered to his nation in the outrage committed on the persons and properties of its subjects, has determined, for the peace and security of the British possessions, and for checking the further progress of this cruel and desolating war, to accede to the prayer of the said Kings, Chiefs and Headmen . . . Wherefore his Excellency Charles Turner . . . on the part and behalf of His Britannic Majesty, and Banka King of Sherbro . . . and Ya Comba, Queen of Ya Comba, by her lawful representatives and next of kin, Thomas Caulker, Chief of Bompay, and George Caulker, Chief of Tasso and the Plantain Isles, with the advice and consent of their tributary Chiefs and Headmen, have mutually agreed . . . for themselves, their tributary Kings, Chiefs and Headmen and people, for them, their heirs and successors, and have forever ceded, transferred amd given over unto said Excellency Charles Turner, Governor of the said colony, their Territories . . . The Governor agrees to accept the cession of the aforesaid Territories and dominions . . . and provide the protection of the British Government, the rights and priviledges of British subjects, and guaranteeing to the said banka, King of Sherbro . . . and to the said Ya Comba, Queen of Ya Comba and her representatives the said Thomas Caulker of Bompay and George Caulker, Chief of Tasso and the Plantain Isles . . . And to their heirs and successors for ever, the full, free, and undisturbed possession and enjoyment of the lands they now hold and occupy.*

Signed at the Plantain Isles on Saturday, the 24th day of September 1825 and ratified in the presence of all the Kings, Chiefs and Headmen of the Sherbro Bulloms at Yoni on Shebro Island, on this 1st day of October, in the year of the Christian era 1825.

Signed by: George Randall, *A.J.C.,* K. Macauley, *M/C . . .* Thomas Caulker, *Chief of Bompay,* George Caulker, *Chief of Tasso and Plantain Isles,* Banka, *King of Sherbro,* Charles Turner, *Govenor of Sierra Leone and Dependencies."*

Proclamation following the ratification : *Now therefore be it known to all whim it may concern, that possession of the said kingdoms has been by us taken in the name and on behalf of His Majesty and that the same, by virtue of the powers in us vested, are constituted an integral part of the colony of Sierra Leone, and are become subject to the navigation and other laws of the mother country and of the said colony.*

Given at Yoni, on Sherbro island, this 3rd day of October 1825". **(Documented in the Sierra Leone Archives, Fourah Bay College)**

Treaty # 39,—July 4th and July 7th 1849—Governor B.C.C.Pine with Canreba Caulker, George Stephen Caulker II Charles Canray, Thomas Stephen Caulker and others. The treaty states that: **"The Caulkers of Shenge/Plantain and the Caulkers of Bompeh should enjoy Tasso as their general burial Ground. The Caulkers of Shenge/Plantain will have jurisdiction as far as Gbarkoh (Cockboro Creek) and the Caulkers of Bompeh will exercise jurisdiction from Karbonko to Ribbi and on to the boundary of the settlement of Sierra Leone. At their death, the chiefdom will be united under a descendant of the late George Stephen Caulker I.**—Referring to the Turner Treaty of 1825. The treaty was ratified at Tasso, the family burial ground.

Treaty # 50—March 31st 1853—**Bompeh, Plantain Islands, and Sherbro Country.**—Anti-slave trade treaty.

Present—Canreba Caulker, Thomas Stephen Caulker and other chiefs of Sherbro, (who sided with the colony against the slave trade) and Govenor A.E. Kennedy. The chiefs had come to Freetown to sign an agreement, promising to maintain their anti-slave-trade engagements. They also signed additional agreements to give up British offenders to the Authorities. The chiefs were given a stipend to make up for losing the sale-trade revenue.

Treaty # 55—April 17th 1854—**Addition to the July 4th treaty of 1849** (see # 39 above)

Treaty # 58—May 31st 1859—**Sherbro Country Annexation**—Commander F.A Close & Thomas Stephen Caulker.

Treaty # 59—June 1st 1859—**Ratification of the May 31st treaty**—Lieutenant T.W. Chapman with Thomas Stephen.

Treaty # 60—June 1st 1859—**Sherbro, Ribbi, Bompeh—Annexation**—Commander F.A.Close and Thomas Stephen Caulker, George Stephen Caulker and Bokari Silly.

Treaty # 66—November 9th—**Sherbro and Turtle islands**—**Annexation**—Governor Stephen John Hill, with Gbana Bome and others,

Treaty # 67—November 9th—**Bendu and Chah Annexation**—Thomas Stephen Caulker and others, with Governor Stephen John Hill—Re: Cession of a portion of Sherbro Country.

Treat # 68—November 9th—**Bagroo Annexation**—Governor Stephen. John Hill with Sei Loko and others—Cession of a portion of the Sherbro country called Bagroo

Treaty # 71—June 11 1870—**The treaty between Bompeh and Plantain**—Governor Arthur Ed. Kennedy C.B. with Thomas Stephen Caulker, Richard Canreba Caulker and others—**Arrangement for adjustment of Dispute.**

Treaty # 72—June 13th 1870—**Plantain and Bompeh**—Governor Arthur kennedy and Thomas Stephen Caulker and others, arrangement for settlement of sucession.—Since the sons of George Stephen Caulker I were all dead, it was decided that the chiefdom would pass to the sons of Thomas Stephen. Richard's chiefdom (Bompeh) would pass to his brothers.

Treaty # 73—June 13th 1870—**Plantain**—Governor Kennedy with Thomas Stephen Caulker—Decision of the Legislative Council as to the succession.

Treaty # 74—June 17th—**Plantain Bompeh**—Governor Kennedy with Thomas Stephen Caulker and others,

Treaty # 82—December 21st 1875—**Bompeh, Sherbro, Bagroo and Taiama**—Governor Sir S. Rowe, with Richard Canreba Caulker—Treaty of Peace.

Treaty # 83—December 21st `875—**Bompeh, Sherbro, Bagroo and Taiama**—Sir S. Rowe, with Chief Richard Canreba—Caulker and others—Treaty of Peace.

Treaty #84—December 30th 1875—**Cockboro and Shenge**—Sir S. Rowe, with George Stephen Caulker II and others.—A Treaty of Peace.

Treaty # 1—December 19th 1881—**Tasso, Plantain, Bompeh, Ribbi**—Governor A.E. Havelock with Thomas Neale—Caulker, Regent of Tasso and Plantain, Richard Canreba Caulker Chief of Bompeh and Ribbi and others. Excerpts read: *"Whereas, by a Convention signed at the Plantain Isles on the 24th day of September 1825 . . . forever ceded, transferred and gave over to His Excellency Charles Turner, . . . Governor-in-chief of the Colony, for the use and on behalf of his majesty the King of Great Britain and Ireland and his successors, the full, entire, free and unlimited right, title, possession and Sovereignty of all the territories and dominions to them respectively belonging, . . . and whereas Charles Turner . . . agreed to accept the cession of the aforesaid territories and the dominions from Banka, King of Sherbro and Ya Comba Queen of Ya Comba . . . we the undersigned, Thomas Neale Caulker Regent Chief of Tasso and the Plantain Isles, Richard Canraybah Caulker, Chief of Bompeh and Ribbee, on the part of our relatives Thomas Caulker and George Caulker, who were parties to the Convention aforesaid, . . . do formally and fully acknowledge and recognize the Sovereignty and rights of Her majest Queen Victoria, herHeirs and Successors, under and by virtue of the aforesaid convention . . . Whereas Her Majesty's Government deems it expedient to continue the payment of stipends to the Chief of Tasso and the Plantain isles and to the Chief of Bompeh and Ribbee, . . . I Arthur Elibank Havelock . . . promise to pay or cause to be paid annually out of the revenues of the Settlement of Sierra Leone to the person for the time being holding during Her Majesty's pleasure, the office of Chief of Tasso and the Plantain Isles, the sum of One hundred pounds; and to the person for the time being holding . . . the office of Chief of Bompeh and Ribbee the sum of Fifty pounds . . .*

The payment of the said stipends and salaries will begin to accrued from the date of the signature of this Declaration and Agreement.

Signed: A.E.Havelock, Governor, Thomas N. Caulker, Regent Chief of Tasso and the Plantain Isles, Richard Canrayba Caulker Chief of Bompeh and Ribbee . . . In the presence of William T.G. Caulker, Thomas E.M. Dillet, Thomas Caulker, Bother of Chief Richard Canrabah Caulker, Jacob W.M.

Lewis—Governor's Clerk." (Documented in the Sierra Leone Archives, Fourah Bay College)

A Memorandum of Agreement : in reference to the Settlement of the dispute between William T.G. Caulker and the late George S. Caulker pf the Plantain Islands, 19th December 1881.

"His Excellency Arthur Elibank Havelock, Esquire, C.M.G. Governor and Commander-in-chief of Her Majesty's West Africa Settlements, having taken into consideration the length of time William T.G. Caulker grandson of George Caulker one of the signitories of General Turner's Treaty dated 14th and 24th September, 1825, has been detained in Freetown, and being desirous that the matter be enquired into and settled, invited the present Regent Chief of the Tasso and the Plantain Islands and the various Chiefs of Bompeh and Ribbee to meet for that purpose.

1. The reason which induced this Government to interfere and rescue William T.G. Caulker in October 1878, when he was in close confinement and ironed, and when the question of putting him to death was under consideration by the late Chief and his advisers, was to prevent the out-break of the war and disturbances in the country which would certainly have followed such a proceeding. The Government commissioned Lieutenant Bright-Smith of the 2nd W.I. Regiment, to proceed to Shaingay to obtain the release of William T.G. Caulker. This was done, and he, William Caulker has been here ever since. The late Chief was urgently requested by the Government to gather the various Chiefs of his District in order to enquire into and settle the matter, but this he had been unable to do up to the day of his death in Freetown on the 2nd of September, 1881.
2. One of the primary charges alleged against William T.G. Caulker was that he assembled a great number of warmen from the Mendi Country to attack the Plantain District; This charge after investigation by His excellency Governor Rowe in 1879 at Sennhoo, and since his departure, has been found to be incorrect.

> The other charges which were preferred against William Caulker were more or less private family matters between him and the late Chief.
>
> 3. The Governor is of opinion that the past should be forgotten and that William T.G. Caulker should now be allowed to return home under the following conditions:-
>
>   1. That he should be given security for good behavior.
>   2. That he should submit himself to the Chiefs appointed to take charge of the Country.
>   3. That he be at liberty to carry on his lawful trade business, and that he should not be molested by anyone; and that all property that may have been taken away from him at the time of or since his arrest by the late Chief be restored to him.
>   4. That should he be aggrieved or unjustly dealt with, he is to report the same to the head Chief, and if no satisfaction be given him, he shall have the right to appeal to the Government for redress.

The above is agreed to by us the undersigned, in token of which we have shaken hands in the presence of the Governor and the assembled Chiefs and Officers, and now attach our signatures.—Thomas N. Caulker, William T.G. Caulker, Momodoo Carimoo—Chief of Bramah, Movee—Chief of Sennehoo, Thoams E.M. Dillet, William S.G. Caulker, A.E. Havelock—Governor, Thos. Geo. Lawson—Government Interpreter, M. Sanusi—Government Arabic Writer.

We the undersigned do swear that the whole of the terms of this Agreement have this day been honestly and truly interpreted by us to the contracting parties, in the Sherbro and mendi languages respectively.

John B. Bowen, Clerk in Holy Orders, N.J. Spain, Extra Clerk.
(Documented in the Sierra Leone Archives, Fourah Bay College)

Appendix VI

The Caulker Manuscripts have been included here, in their original language. The original document seems to have disappeared from the Sierra Leone Archives, yet it is important for us as a family, to know what they contained. This document has been retyped by Issatu Karefa-Smart

The Caulker Manuscripts

By George Maximillan Domingo
Taken From Sierra Leone Studies
Part 1—October 1920 pp 28-48
Part II—July 1925 pp 1-18

GEORGE MAXIMILLAN DOMINGO
SPEAKER TO MADAM SOPHIA N. CAULKER
Paramount Chief of Shengeh

CHARLES WALTERSON DOMINGO
Late of
COLONIAL SECRETARIAT
NIGERIA

The Causes of the wars

I am going to give a short history in this little book, about the causes of the wars within the Caulker Family. First, I will try to explain the causes of the war between Thomas Stephen Caulker Regent of Shengeh/Plantain and Charles Caulker chief of Bompeh, which occurred about the middle of the nineteenth century.

George Stephen Caulker, alias Bah Charch, was one of the children of Stephen Caulker, who was paramount chief of all of Bompeh, Shengeh and Plantain Districts between 1799-1810.

On his return from school in England, Stephen's son George had asked his uncle Thomas Kon Tham who had succeeded Stephen as chief in 1810, to give him part of the chiefdom to rule. His uncle agreed and gave him the Shengeh and Plantain district.

During George's lifetime he had a son named Thomas Koogbah Caulker, alias Bahome Koogbah, several daughters and a brother named Thomas Stephen Caulker, also known as Bah Tham. When George died in October, 1831, his brother Thomas Stephen Caulker (Ba Tham) was made regent chief, because his brother George's son Thomas Koogbah Caulker was not yet of age and his other children were girls.

When chief Thomas Kon Tham died in 1832, he was succeeded by his brother Charles (also known as Ba Charley). A quarrel arose between the servants of Thomas Stephen Caulker of Plantain and the servants of Charles of Bompeh. It was alleged that Thomas Stephen's servants were spreading rumors about the chiefdom of Bompeh and saying the late Thomas Caulker (Kon Tham of Bompeh, had a son named Canray Bah by a woman of Gbambahyah and was being raised by his maternal uncle at Gbambahyah.

At this time Thomas Stephen Caulker who was living with his elder brother George Stephen (Ba Charch) now chief of Plantain/Shengeh, had been serving his brother in different capacities. This time, Thomas had been sent on an errand to Gbanbahyah, where he found Canray Ba Caulker, who was said to be a son of his cousin, Thomas Caulker (Kon Tham). After this discovery, he observed the usual native ceremony, in order that his young cousin could be given to him. His request was granted and he was able to bring the young man home to the Plantain Island.

From there Canrayba was sent to his father in Bompeh. When Thomas Kon Tham died in 1832, this young man was looked upon by the people as the 'Crown Prince of the Bompeh District', although Charles Caulker, (Ba Charlay) had been elected chief over the Bompeh District. Charles' chieftaincy was seen as a nominal affair; for Canreba the perceived Crown Prince, was really the power behind the throne. Since this aspersion was cast on the chiefdom of Bompeh, Canreba Caulker had been trying to talk his uncle Charles into not to accepting such an insult, but rather to avenge it in some way. His uncle agreed to declare war with the Caulkers of Shengeh and Plantain Districts. As an adviser, Canreba also suggested to his (uncle) that he had a better claim to the chieftaincy of Shengeh than his cousin Thomas Stephen, and that the many gifts which had been sent to him from time to time by his cousin were not really gifts, but had rightly belonged to him. He felt that they should take up arms at once and wrest the chiefdom of Shengeh from Thomas Stephen.

Keep in mind that this adviser, Canreba Caulker, was raised at Gbambayah among a warlike people, and he was of the same disposition as a native of that country.

So, Ba Charley Caulker and his nephew, began making preparations to invade Plantain and Shengeh. When the news reached Thomas Stephen, he too began making preparations immediately, so that he could defend his chiefdom. He considered himself the rightful heir to the chiefdom over which he was ruling and claimed that he was the one who had served under the late George Stephen Caulker during his lifetime and George was his brother. Besides that, it was he and his late brother George Stephen Caulker who were instrumental in getting Canreba Caulker to Bompeh. For these reasons he had more rights over Plantain and Shengeh and the Bompeh District than those of any other living man in the family. So he continued to make big plans for the defense of his chiefdom. But the war did not take place as was anticipated, because the sub-chief of Ribbee, which was then under the chieftaincy of Bompeh, Thethah Yangkie interfered and called a meeting of the two chiefs for peace talks.

It was agreed that a place be appointed where both parties could meet and come to terms of peace. It was customary in those days, in case of a tribal dispute, for one or two chiefs to call the disputing parties together to settle their differences. About the year 1799 the only paramount chieftaincy on this side of the coast of Sierra Leone was that of the Caulkers of Plantain and Shengeh Districts and the Bompeh. So the meeting would be between the two Caulker chiefdoms. Ribbee was the place chosen. In many cases the planners of these meetings proved to be traitors, as it was in this case. I am sorry to say that although the action of the sub-chief of Ribbee seemed to a good one, It was a very treacherous and deceptive act.

The men of Ribbee and Bompeh, as well as the Caulkers of Bompeh were Porroh men, and Porroh is considered a society of peace. The sub-chief, Pah Kainey of Ribbee and Ba Charlay chief of Bompeh, had jointly planned a war against Thomas Stephen Caulker under the guise of Porroh, which they secretly hid in a town called Ngbahsahthee in the frontier of the Ribbee. They summoned the chief of Shengeh to a meeting of the chiefs at Ribbee so that they could talk peace. The Caulkers of Shengeh were not Porroh men at the time, nor did they suspect that this was a treacherous call. The chief of Plantain and Shengeh and his people agreed to obey the call. So they went to Ribbee in State.

They traveled by sea in one of the royal cutters. They embarked in the morning and arrived at the mouth of the Ribbee River where they anchored and waited for the other boats which were bringing the sub-chiefs from Plantain and Shengeh districts, in the afternoon,. Amongst the boats which arrived, were some which belonged to Thomas Koogbah Caulker, son of the late George Stephen, for whom Thomas Stephen Caulker was acting as regent, Yah Coomba of Tasso, Yorgbor of Bendoo, Yah Bome of Thoombah, Sopolee of Konnohloh and Sosanthee of Cargbor River and several others. They were all cordially welcomed and quarters were provided for them in the southern part of town. Since this was a treacherous act, the hosts thought it best to house them there, so that none would escape when the diabolical act was carried out. They were satisfied that it was a well-laid plot. As was customary, the chief of Plantain and Shengeh made the usual ceremony, which was accepted. A day was appointed for settling of the differences between the two parties. The matter of the plot was to be kept a secret and was not to be disclosed to any one from Plantain and Shengeh Districts, be he a Porroh man or a not.

Dancing began immediately and continued for three successive days, during which time people came in great numbers from all parts of Ribbee, Bompeh, Cammaranca, Yonnie and Mende, with weapons of war, such as matchet-blades, sword-blades and flint-lock guns. They hid themselves and their weapons in the Porroh bush waiting for the orders to strike the chief and his people from Plantain and Shengeh Districts. One of the secrets of the plot was to kill the chief of Shengeh and his followers, and immediately send troops by sea to invade Plantain and Shengeh Districts. Charles Caulker, and Canreba Caulker then planned to establish themselves as paramount chiefs over Bompeh, Plantain and Shengeh Districts. They were determined to do this, because Stephen Caulker (Thomas Stephen's father) had previously gained possession of the Banana Islands by conquest many years ago and had established himself as 'The re-conqueror of The Banana Islands', and Charles wanted to do the same.

As providence would have it, the plot was disclosed. There was a man from Ribbee who had previously lived at Bompeh. His name was Bureh Warkree and he was a Porroh man. He had a daughter by the name of Yah Concheh, who had been the wife of the late George Stephen Caulker, brother of Thomas Stephen against whom this plot was made. It meant death to disclose the secrets of Porroh, but in spite of this, Bureh Warkree sacrificed his life and reported the plot to Thomas Stephen saying that, if he (the chief) and his followers waited till the "Lackah" (an officer of the Porroh) came out, he and his people would be massacred. He urged the chief to leave stealthily and instantly. This information put the chief on his guard. He called his officers privately and gave them the information. He and his officers summoned the courage, and secretly managed to get the young men and women into the small boats, drifted them down on the river and got into the cutter. The chief disguised himself, walked in the mud among the black mangrove trees and was carried into his cutter. When it was discovered that the chief and his people had escaped, the hosts called a meeting of the people and accused Bureh Warkree of disclosing their plot. Since he was a relative of the Caulkers of Plantain and Shengeh, he was found guilty. The penalty was death and his throat was cut. In order to carry out their plan, they immediately dispatched their war boys to Plantain Island to besiege it. Shengeh was then only a small village, whilst the Plantain Island was a large town and the home of the Caulker family.

When the war boys reached Plantain Island however, the chief, was not there. As soon as he had made his escape safely and arrived at home, the next day he ordered all the young children to be moved to Daymah Islands in care of Lucia San Bokrah. Some of the children included:—Sophia Caulker (later Sophia Neale Caulker), Neker Caulker, Lucia Caulker, Yah Bendoo, Koombah Caulker and Susannah Caulker. After the children had been taken to safety, the chief proceeded to Yainkain to lodge a complaint to the chief Bah Ville about what his cousins Charles Caulker and Canre Bah had planned. He then went to Bendoo, (now known as British Bendoo, Sherbro) with the same complaint to the chief Lango Bah Colboa. While he was in Bendoo he heard the booming of guns and knew that the Plantain Island had been taken.

Although the town was walled and well fortified with a cannon already loaded for action at any time, when the enemy came they met with very little resistance as the main body of Thomas' warriors had been sent overland from Shengeh to Mocaibay to prevent the enemy from coming over to the Island. The chief had taken the best of the warriors along with him to Yainkain and Bendoo. The enemy came by sea from Ribbee and Bompeh in the Harmattan season when it was foggy, which gave them the advantage to arrive without being detected. The town was besieged, stormed and taken. Two people were killed and the rest mostly women of the Caulker family, were taken prisoner. Charles Caulker and Canray Bah Caulker had given orders to their warriors, if they succeeded in taking any of the female members of the Caulker's family prisoner, they were not to be treated roughly. They were to be tied with head kerchiefs not ropes. The males in the family who offered no resistance were not to be killed. Instead, they were to be brought to them. The other captives, including the boatmen, who were partially the cause of the war and who were not of the family were to be killed.

Thomas Stephen Caulker returned from Yainkain and Bendoo only to find his town on Plantain Island in ashes. With those whom he could find in the town, he decided to return to Bendoo.

Immediately after Plantain Island was burned, Chief Charles Caulker and Canreba Caulker sent their armies all round the various towns, to such places as Gborkor, Rembee, Yandoo, Mambo and all up and down the Cargbor River, Thaimdale and lower Bagroo, Bambahyah, Daymah, Sacheeh, Bonthe, Nongoobah Bolom, Boom River and Bawhall, and forced the people to join them in continuing the war. The only chiefdoms which remained allies to Thomas Stephen Caulker were Mongray under chief Kiskammah and Mano Bagroo under chief Sehy Keah Bokah.

Although Thomas Stephen was responsible for sending Thomas Koogba and his cousin Charles to Freetown, where they got a good education, Thomas Koogba was very hostile towards his uncle. They returned home just about the time the quarrel between the Bompeh Caulkers and Plantain/Shengeh Caulkers was starting and instead of joining their uncle, both of them joined their cousin in Bompeh, Canreba, who was now fighting alone. The year was 1842, and Chief Charles Caulker had died. Thomas and Charles were made generals in Canreba's army to fight against their uncle and benefactor, Thomas Stephen Caulker.

Thomas Koogbah Caulker who lived in Mambo in the Plantain and Shengeh Districts, went from there and built a town which he named Sinclair, (now known to mariners as Buoy Point in the Sherbro River). This he planned to use as a garrison. He changed his own name to Masso, a name commonly associated with the highest officer of the Bundu Society who it was said, always got her newly initiated candidates out in the early morning. He took that name because, like the Masso, Thomas planned to collect his war boys from Ribbee all the way down to the Imperreh, and march them to Bendoo early in the morning and take the town without any struggle. He went over to Daymah and forced the inhabitants to join him in the fight against his uncle and made his cousin Charles Marlehlow their general.

Thomas Stephen Caulker was now at Bendoo, a stranger in a strange land, with only a few men. His son George Stephen II who was named after his brother George Stephen Caulker I had been in school in England for seven years. On his return home he went to Matacong in the Northern Rivers (now known as French Guinea), to gain more experience so that, in the event he became a chief, he would be qualified for such an office, in much the same way David, the shepherd boy, who was anointed as the next king of Israel, learned as much as he could in preparation for the high office of king he later was to have. If one wants to be a ruler, one should not spend the time in idleness but, after gaining all the book knowledge that is possible, one should go into some other country and prepare for such an office. So young George Stephen Caulker went to Matacong, where the sad news of the war against his father and the fall of Plantain Island reached him. *(Matacong was ceded to Britain in 1826 (Treaty No. 15) and transferred to France in 1829)*

Imagine the difficulty he must have had trying send a message to his father. French Guinea was no longer a British territory, no steamer was running between here and the Northern River; the Caulkers of Bompeh, who were the enemy, were on their way to Bendoo, and Thomas Koogbah Caulker was at Buoy Point. Communication between father and son was indeed impossible. When matters came to a head, some men volunteered and went with one of the merchant schooners to Freetown, where they were able to get passage to Benty and on to young Prince Caulker in Matacong.

Meanwhile, although Thomas Stephen Caulker, was a stranger at Bendoo, he was not idle. He had been busy asking neighboring chiefs for help with his troubles—asking for war boys to assist in driving his enemies from the territory. In many instances he was refused, but succeeded in getting some from in only two chiefs. He got help from Kiskammah chief of Mongray and Sehy Keah Bokkah, chief of Mano Bagroo. Iudisson, chief of York Island, was neutral in the matter.

Canray Bah Caulker and Thomas Koogbah Caulker on the other hand, had been mustering war boys from all parts of the countries where they had forced people to be loyal to them. These war boys had been collected at Bachuhland and at Bonthe. They planned to march over to Bendoo and invade it without a struggle as Masso had said. The preparations on both sides took about a year.

Thomas Stephen Caulker had built stockades for defense at Bendoo, and had moved the inhabitants of the adjacent and remote villages into Bendoo. He was privileged to have been supplied with head warriors such as Mannnah Fallah, Jangah and a few war boys who were to man the stockades.

Canreba Caulker and Thomas Koogbah had crossed from Bonthe with a large number of war boys and built four stockades inland around the stockade which Thomas Stephen had built. As the latter felt that he had not yet collected enough war boys, he offered no resistance. This gave the enemy the opportunity to plunder whatever they could find in the deserted villages.

The messengers who had been sent to the Northern rivers, returned and reported to Thomas Stephen that his son was sending him help in a schooner which he had chartered from Mr. Isaacs. Sehy Keah Bokah, chief of Mano Bagroo, also honored Thomas Stephen's request by sending him a good number of old experienced war boys who were very courageous. They were headed by a warrior named Yah Gbarmah Yehkeh. The supply of war boys which was expected from the Northern rivers came by schooner with a brave and daring warrior named Jongah, alias Thomas Nightingale, a native of Rio Pongas. They brought with them gunpowder, guns and sword blades and stores.

This strengthened Thomas Stephen forces. Jongah was a brave and daring warrior as we shall find in his heroic-exploits during the war. He came at an opportune time, just when Canray Bah and Thomas Koogbah were preparing to invade Bendoo.

In native wars, the war boys do not carry stores. They take whatever they can find by plundering. Since they had used everything they had found in the deserted villages, they thought it was high time they struck the first blow. During this interval, Masso himself was still in his garrison at Buoy Point. His cousin Charles, alias Kawgbandee, was in charge of the war boys at Bonthe. (He named himself Kawgbandee as the one who would inspire the whole army of war boys to action.) Kehkehgbookeh, a man of extraordinary size and Kehkendo were the chief warriors in charge of the war boys in the four stockades which they had built around Bendoo. Kehkehgbookeh sent a message to Masso saying that they were quite ready for action and had filled much of the Bendoo land. There still a great number of war boys at Bonthe. They were self-confident that their numbers were sufficient. and according to standards of military strength, efficient enough to obtain victory without any struggle. They were only waiting for his arrival.

But Thomas Stephen became sick, suffering from a boil under his arm. One day Masso, who had arrived at Bonthe, sent word to his chief warriors asking them to inform his uncle that, he was to save a portion of whatever he had eaten for dinner, so that he would have food in the morning, when he expected to cross over and march his army into Bendoo.

Bendoo was well fortified with well trained warriors in charge of the stockades. They were Saw Party, alias Mbongoombah, *(meaning "shoots him on the head."—a Mende word indicating a good marksman)* Saisay Marthee, alias Teweh Ndia, *(meaning "cuts him in two,"—a mende word which literally means 'cut-middle')* and Jangah, father of Maria Jangah, alias Mrs. Maria Newland now of Kereh-keh, Mye in Plantain and Shengeh Districts and Fatomah, now of Gaindamah. The Mongray chief had also promised reinforcements to Thomas Stephen in case of emergency, and as the war was about to begin, he sent Mannah Fallah, one of his chief warriors, to head the reinforcements and bring them down. It was during Manna Fallah's absence that the order for the war to begin was given.

The notorious morning dawned, and I am glad to say that Bendoo was not attacked at night, as is customary in native wars, because the enemy were confident that in their war, they could make the attack so easily at any time. The war boys who were at Bonthe got into canoes headed by Kawgbandee and Masso himself. There were about 150 canoes approaching Bendoo.

Thomas Stephen's war boys were also prepared for battle. When all was ready he addressed his men as follows: "Go! I have done nothing wrong; it is an unrighteous war against me and God will deliver them into your hands!"

Jongah, (aka Thomas Nightingale) was sitting in a Kroo canoe of twelve paddles and rowers back to back so that he would be able to go forward or backwards without having the paddles removed. A bugler by the name William Domingo, alias Sangoi, father of the writer, J. Wallestain Domingo of San Domingo, Charles W. Domingo of the Secretariat, Lagos, and Henry Domingo of Matadi, in the Congo Free State, also accompanied him.

Before pushing off to meet the enemy, Jongah said that if one of the enemy was able, during the attack, to cross over and come to Bendoo and conquer it, Thomas Stephen Caulker could take Rio Pongas—Jongah's own country, instead. Jamga of Mongray also said, if he failed to defend the stockade and allowed one of the enemy to come into it, he would give Mongray instead.

A Mohammedan priest was seen coming out of the stockade in which Kehkehgbookeh the chief warrior of the Bompeh side was assigned, with a tassabeah (*Rosary beads*) in his hand. He was praying for the success of his people. Moongoombah *("shot him on the head," as his name means)*, shot him in the head and he fell dead.

After this, Kehkehgbookeh and his warriors marched manfully to the stockade of Bendoo and tried to force entrance by chopping their way in. They succeed in cutting a hole through which they would gain entrance, but they were forced to leave due to the prompt action of Jangah who was in charge of this stockade. Kehkehgbookeh and his boys went to another part of the stockade and tried to gain entrance there by leaping over the wall. They had almost succeeded, when the reinforcements from Kiskammah arrived. The chief warriors in the reinforcements were Bainjaka, Borbor, Baing and Armodu Fullehy of Kangamah. The enemy, on realizing that these were reinforcements, shot at them and Mannah Fallah, one of the chief warriors from Mongray, was shot on the nose. Mannah Fallah was enraged. He chased the enemy and killed many of them. Still, the fighting continued and Kehkehbookeh, being an experience warrior, was still boasting, when, like Goliath of Gath, he was shot down by Saw Party. Seeing their leader down, the enemy fled but were pursued. A very great many were slaughtered.

Remember that we had left Jongah, alias Nightingale, his bugler Sangoi, and a handful of men, at sea facing over a hundred and fifty canoes of the enemy at the Bendoo bay. It 's hard to believe, although it is a fact, that thousands of those in the canoes were slain that day. Some were thrown into the water and were drowned and the creeks and rivulets were filled with dead bodies which became a feast for the fishes and alligators. Masso, now defeated, sought refuge at York Island. Kawgbandee, the head warrior, who was in charge of the garrison at Bonthe, had been taken captive but because of the clemency granted by his uncle, Thomas Stephen, he was set free much to the vexation of Thomas Stephen's war boys, who said Kawgbandee deserved nothing but death. Surprisingly, Thomas Stephen Caulker's maternal uncles Gbannah Barcoo and Canray Dow, were also taken captive. Both of them had been sub-chiefs of Bendoo, Thoombah, Shengeh District, the birthplace of Thomas Stephen Caulker's mother. They were queried as to the reason why they had taken up arms against their nephew. They replied that they had been forced to do so. Thomas Stephen ordered them to be killed lest they remain and sow the seeds of discord in the family.

After the battle of that day, the war boys cut off the heads of the enemy who had been killed on land, piled them up in a great heap about six feet high and about twelve feet around. Some of the skulls were hung up on the branches of large thorny trees to represent their fruit. There are a few scattered ones on the spot until this day.*(at the time the book was written)*

One of the captives, a singer who was a native of Sacheeh, pleaded that his life be spared. When he was asked why he took part in the war, he said he did it simply to save his life. He was asked to sing a few of his native songs. The war boys were satisfied with his performance, and he was released. The chief told him to go home and tell his people that he had done nothing wrong, and that God had helped to defeat his enemies. After some time the man returned in a canoe which carried some of the elderly people from his village. They had come to place themselves under the protection of Thomas Stephen Caulker. The reason the man gave for this request was that after he had been leased, enemy troops had gone to Yonnie, Mosolo, Bonthe and other villages killing the people, plundering, and taking as many captives as they could find. Some of his people took refuge in his home, when they realized that troops would ransack all the corners of Sherbro Island. So he came over with the elderly people of this village so that they could be under the protection of this powerful chief, against the invasion of Canreba Caulker or any other tribe or chief. To show their loyalty, they gave him a wife—a daughter of one of their chiefs. When she was accepted, they were sure that they would be safe from any invader.

Masso had left York Island where he first took refuge and came to Sahn in the Thaimdale District. He hid here for sometime, leaving some of his chief warriors who had escaped death, at Buoy Point. He also tried as best as he could to raise more war boys.

Thomas Stephen Caulker was now determined to punish the people of those chiefdoms and districts who had assisted his cousin and nephews in the war against him. He recalled his troops from the Sherbro Island and dispatched Johgah, Mannah Fallah, and Jangah as chief warriors, to Tasso, Shengeh District, Bainjak, Gerindeah and Borbor. Armodu Foolehy with Fahgbannah Yeh Keh were to go to Mambo, Mano Bagroo and all along the coast. From lower Bagroo to Cargbor, from Mambo on to the head of the Cargbor River. Both columns were to meet up and conquer all the way to Bendoo. They were to punish the inhabitants, by killing, plundering and taking as many captives as they chose. Since these columns would pass through Thaimdale where Thomas Koogbah Caulker, (Masso), was in hiding, he fled and sought refuge in the Kittam River knowing that he would not be strong enough to resist their attack. His chief warrior and cousin Charles (Kawgbandee, who had fought with him against their uncle) fled to the Bompeh District and took refuge at Mo-Torbon. While Thomas Koogbah and Charles were in exile William Caulker, *(the author of the raid of 1887 to be discussed later)*, was born to Thomas Koogbah Caulker and. Kawgbandee got himself a wife and they had a son named Charles Caulker, aka. Marlehow.

While Thomas Koogbah Caulker was a refugee at the Kittam River he sent ambassadors to his uncle Thomas Stephen who was then still at Bendoo to beg for forgiveness and secure peace. His uncle would not have forgiven such an ungrateful and treacherous nephew, but his daughters begged for their cousin. When the message reached Masso that he had been pardoned by his uncle, he could not believe it. So when chief Mannah of Gallinas was going on a 'State visit' to Thomas Stephen, Thomas Koogbah (Masso) accompanied the chief, to make sure that his forgiveness had been real.

For many years, things remained peaceful and Thomas Stephen Caulker grew strong. He collected more war boys and sent them up as far as the mouths of the Boom and Kittam Rivers and subdued those countries. After a while, he collected more troops because he wanted to invade Bompeh, just as they had done to him. But rumors of these preparations created great panic in the Bompeh territory, even though Canreba Caulker had made his own ample preparations for defence. The southern district was also disturbed by Canreba's preparations and refugees poured into the settlement from all quarters. The situation caused a great setback to the Timber trade in this part of the country, for timber was the main product of trade, which was exported to England in great quantities from the Bompeh and Shengeh Districts. When matters became too serious and interfered with the other interests of the Colony proper, the traders, through a Mr. Lemon, reported the situation to the then Governor, Colonel George Macdonald, who wrote to Thomas Stephen Caulker of Shengeh and Canreba Caulker of Bompeh asking them to meet with him for peace talks. In reply both chiefs agreed to a meeting. But Thomas Stephen, who was then at Bendoo, refused to go to Bompeh and Canreba, who was then at Bompeh, refused to go to Bendoo. The Governor then chose Tasso as the meeting place, to which they both consented. During this meeting the Treaty of 1845 was drawn up stating the terms of peace.

The Treaty of 1845—*"The Caulkers of Shengeh and the Caulkers of Bompeh will enjoy Tasso as their general burying place. The Caulkers of Shengeh will exercise jurisdiction as far as Gbarkoh creek, alias Karbonko, and the Caulkers of Bompeh will exercise jurisdiction from the Karbonko on the Ribbee and on to the boundary of the settlement of Sierra Leone".*

Both chiefs agreed to the treaty.

Thomas Stephen Caulker returned to Bendoo and Canreba Caulker to Bompeh. Since then, both chiefs have continued to exercise jurisdiction over their respective chiefdoms undisturbed.

Although both chiefdoms were relatively quiet, and there were no hostilities between the two chiefs, there was great animosity between their offspring and many tribal disputes between the natives themselves, especially those from Bagroo to the lower part of the Shengeh District. Thomas Stephen grew stronger by his conquests and was highly honored by all the other chiefs who looked up to him as their superior. Even the once notable chief Mannah of Gaindamah, Gallinas country came to pay him a special visit.

Canreba Caulker was no less strong at Bompeh and was highly honored by the surrounding chiefs and headmen. During the preparations he had been making previously for defense, when he had to get war boys, he had succeeded in getting Sorie Kehsebeh, a once notable Lokkoh warrior, and the Lokkohs to come down to Bompeh. After the terms of peace, he offered them the town of Rotifunk with its suburbs, so that they could stay there incase of any emergency and therefore be available to help.

There is a story told of Canray Bah Caulker, which the natives believe to be true. One day, a timber trading vessel arrived in Bompeh and after loading it with timber, Canreba went on board as a visitor. As soon as he boarded the vessel, it leaned on one side to such an extent that the captain exclaimed "Hallo, Caulker, do you want to sink my ship?" since then the natives regarded him as an extraordinary individual with supernatural powers. Immediately after this, incident, Canreba began building of a stone house which he did not finish. The ruins of the house can be seen to this day at Bompeh.

Canray Bah Caulker is still considered the mightiest ruler Bompeh ever had, even though he had educated sons who later became his successors. His reign lasted about twenty-five years and he died in 1857, leaving behind his sons Richard Canreba Caulker, Thomas Canreba Caulker and others. He was succeeded by his brother Theophilus Caulker, alias Thambum, the father of James Canreba Caulker, who became paramount chief in 1899 and died in 1902. John Canreba Caulker, another son of Thambum, became paramount chief in 1902 and died in 1907.

Thomas Stephen Caulker survived has cousin Canreba Caulker and was still at Bendoo. Some of his people had returned home and re-peopled Shengeh but not Plantain. The principal ones among those who returned to Shengeh were Beah Will, Thethan Yang Sally, mother of William (Willie) Caulker, the first cabinet-maker of Shengeh, and Thethan Yang Kate, a sister of the chief and Thethah Yang Maligah.

This ends the war known as Stephen Caulker and Canreba's war or "Pemm Sabbah" as known by the natives. Jongah, Mannah Fallah, Jangah and other chief warriors were still with Thomas Stephen Caulker at Bendoo making Sinclair his headquarters where he established himself and exerted much influence over the people of those parts. They honored him and remained loyal to him.

The story of Masso (Thomas Koogba) getting a second wife from the people of Thaimdale goes like this: Kong Gborgbor, who of late was known as Kong Doomhbay, was not a native of either Bompeh or Shengeh District, but came from the Boom River as a refugee. Because of his continued expertise as a warrior, he found favor with the people and also with Masso who had established himself as a chieftain over the people. Kong Gborgbor advised the people of Thaimdale that if they wanted to gain the good wishes of Masso and free themselves from the frequent plunder and marauding of the war boys, they should find a young lady of excellent beauty and present her as a wife to Masso. This advice was considered wise and so a daughter of one of the chiefs was secured and sent by Kong Doomahbey the special messenger. The new wife was accepted and she became the mother of Francis Theophilus Caulker, the present sub-chief of Mambo, Shengeh District. Kong Doomahbey was now taken into confidence and favor by both Masso and the people. Masso ceased hostility with the people of Thaimdale and turned his attention to passers-by. His war boys were used to plunder those of the Bagroo, Daymah, Imperreh and Shengeh Districts and any boats and canoes passing at sea. This way of plundering brought about the capture of the late Canray Sammamish, his mother and brothers who were on their way to Freetown from the Gallinas. The raids continued until Thomas Koogbah, because of ill-health, had to leave Thaimdale for Mambo on the Cargbor River. He left the district in charge of Kohg Doomahbey who, by his prowess, established himself as paramount chief over all the other chiefs. As he grew strong in power so he grew wicked. In those dark and war-like days he would for a very trifling offence put an end to a man's life. He proved so vicious and wicked that the natives changed his name from Kong. Gborgbor to Kong Doomahbey, which means wicked Kong. This Kong Doomahbey was the father of the late Alexander Doomahbey, who was hanged for participating in the raid of 1898, Jabez Doomahbey, now of Northern Nigeria, and Isreal Doomahbey (who had received a death sentence which was later commuted to life imprisonment). He later died in the Freetown jail. John Doommahbey, who as hanged for cannibalism in 1907, and Flora Doomahbey who now lives at Mambo.

Thomas Koogbah Caulker recovered from his illness shortly after he returned home to Mambo and lived until his death in 1868, several years after his uncle Thomas Stephen had returned to Shengeh. He was generally known by the name of Masso rather than by Thomas Koogbah Caulker. When he died he was interred at Tassoh, where a tombstone was erected over his grave by his son William.

CAULKER MANUSCRIPTS

Part II
William Caulker

After being well established, William Caulker made friends in the Bullom country, and visited them frequently. He often traveled with two or three boys or girls, and sometimes returned with only one child. But no one dared question him about the children, or, if any one had the audacity to ask him what had happened to the children, he would tell them that the children had been left with his wives' relatives. This situation continued for about three years.

Eventually, some strangers came to him from the Soosoo country. When they were ready to return he gave them ten boys and girls. The children were taken overland, whilst he and his cousin, Charles Marlehlow Caulker, traveled by sea. When the parents of these children, saw this, all of them went to the Regent chief, Thomas Neal Caulker, and informed him that William Caulker had sent ten of their children to the northern rivers to be sold. The chief replied that he had not known when the children were given to William Caulker so, he had nothing to do with it. The parents told the chief that they had been forced to do so. They would not have objected if the children were working for Mr. Caulker where they could see them. When the chief, saw the anxiety and pitiful condition of the parents, he addressed a letter to the chief of Bompeh District and asked him not to allow the Soosoo strangers to pass through with those children. He then boarded his boat and waited at the mouth of the Cockboro river for William Caulker. That night, as William was arriving at Tassoh to pay homage to his ancestors before he proceeded on his journey; he was arrested and brought to Shengeh. He was queried about his action, and he pleaded guilty to the charge and admitted that he was going to sell them. He was asked to confirm his testimony by signing his name and he said he would think about it, but before he did so, his men must be allowed to return home. This was granted. The men went home . . . while William was detained. After a few days he himself escaped. They search high and low for him, and since they could not find him, the children were returned to their parents, and the matter was forwarded to the Colonial Government.

After this event, William renewed his friendship with S.B.A. Macfoy, a trader from Jamaica, who began to supply him with goods with which he ran a small business at Mambo. With the help of his wives and servants and his wives' relatives, he was making a living. He was a man who knew how to make friends, and so he had a lot of friends from different places.

William had given some land in a town called Maneah, to a Mohammedan man, who had become his friend. William was now his landlord. This man had a boy whom he was teaching Arabic.

Porroh was then in session at Mokainey and this boy happened to come in contact with the members and he was taken and initiated. The boy's master then took his cutlass and went into the porroh bush determined to get his boy back. He was caught and detained by the Porroh members. When William, who himself was not a porroh man, heard about this, he was very angry and went to the porroh men, demanding the boy and his Mahommedian stranger. The porroh men, in turn demanded that a fine be paid by him because the stranger had violated the porroh law by going into the bush. As for the boy, he had received the penalty due to him and it was not possible for him to return until the porroh session was over. William Caulker did not agree with this. He said that the law of the country was that, if the stranger of any individual violated any of the laws of the country, it was the duty of the offendedr to first inform the landlord about the offence before steps were taken. Therefore he would not pay anything but demand that his strangers be returned. This created a lot of unrest, till the matter was brought before the Regent Chief, Thomas Neale Caulker. The Chief, not being a porroh man, could not decide the case, although he advised William to give up the case especially as his stranger had taken up arms against the porroh—the highest society of peace in the country. Since William would not listen to his advise, the chief was obliged to forward the matter to the British Government which took up the case. Since William had renewed his friendship with Mr. S.B.A Macfoy, Macfoy backed him and procured him the assistance of a lawyer in the person of Samuel Lewis, Esq., who defended William brilliantly case and received judgment. The lawyer then warned him to be cautious, for he had only escaped by the skin of his teeth. It would have been better for William if he had been found guilty and sent to prison, for he would not have had the liberty to bring about the raid of 1887 which ended his life on the gallows. When he returned to Mambo, his stranger and the boy had been returned to him without any fine.

Around this time there was a war in Kittam and all the traders were forced to leave the country. Since William Caulker was a native of that country, Mr. Macfoy had the advantage of using him as a trader there, and continued using his services until a long boat, well laden with goods of over £500 value, was plundered by the warriors at Barthahol. William Caulker and the crew had a narrow escape. When the report reached Mr. Macfoy, he claimed William was responsible for the loss, since he had assured Macfoy that he was from the Kittam and his goods were safe in his hands. William accepted the blame and promised to pay the amount lost in two years. He returned to his home at Mambo and did all he could to settle the debt. But although he lived five years after this event, he failed in his attempt to pay the debt. Although Mr. Macfoy did not press him for payment of the debt, they were no longer on good terms of friendship. During William's absence from home, two of the boys whom he had tried to sell off to the Soosoo country, violated two of his wives. When he found out about the incident, William promised to deal with them accordingly, since they had refused to work for him. When their parents heard about his plan, they took the boys and fled to Mudli Sesil for protection. Mudli was afraid to approach William on this matter and so took a head of Money (£3) and came to the chief Thomas Neale Caulker begging him for protection for these people. The chief, after receiving the head of money, told Mudli that he had a case against William Caulker and ordered him to Shengeh. Franklin Caulker, brother of Thomas Neale was present when this order was given, and he went and told William of it, warning him to beware of Mudli Sesil.

When he heard about the possible danger, William took all of his wives to Tanganemah where he hid them, and then went to Richard Canray Bah Caulker to complain of Thomas Neale's plan. He also said that he was going to Nooghahmah of Patafu and Kaingambomeh of Moyamba to ask for some people to accompany him to get revenge against those who had violated his wives. Richard Caulker asked him not to go but suggested he wait for him to send to the chief of Shengeh and see if his case could be adjusted. Next morning, whilst they were preparing breakfast, William who was pretending to wait for the tide, left and went to the Mende country where he met a man called Ndambah who also had some ill-feelings against the Shengeh chief, He asked William to join him so that he could get revenge. This man who was a native of the Mende country, had more influence with his people and through him, William Caulker succeeded in his talks with the Mende chiefs, from whom he got war boys to come down with him. The chiefs who assisted him were Noogbahman, Tarcoyo, Konjo, Kehngeebomeh. William was supplied with such a large number of war boys, he could only bring one-forth of them, and planned to ask Ndambah to bring the rest if they were needed.

He and his war boys traveled down to Bompeh District and caused no disturbance on the way. Neither were they troubled by anyone, until they reached Shengeh District. They entered Larwahnah on 24th May, 1887. This is the town where Mudli Sesil who had been ordered to arrest William lived. At the time, it was the richest town in the district. Here they plundered everything they could find. During the plunder Yafodu a townsman, tried to resist but was killed by the roadside. Another man named Murry, escaped to the bush with some people. But Mudli, some of his wives and the rest of those who had remained were caught. This was the fall of Larwahnah and she never again rose to her former state.

The next day William marched his war boys to Mambo, seized those who had violated his wives and put them in chains, but did no harm to the Mambo mission or missionaries. If he had meant war, he could have marched into Shengeh without any resistance. Had he not followed the evil counsel of others, he might still have been alive. He stopped in Mambo which was his home, but the news of his arrival with war boys from the Mende Country and the plunder of Larwahnah, the killing of Yafoday, and the capture of so many others, put the country in great panic. The inhabitants began to seek refuge in the colony, Daymah, Thaimdale and Bonthe. On the 27th of May, Canray Phemah of Mothinkle went to William and told him that he was dissatisfied with the decision that chief Thomas Neale of Shengeh had given in his case and so would join him to get revenge. But William told him that he had done what he intended and had no plans to do anything else, unless he was troubled again. He also said that if things continued to be peaceful he would send some of the war boys back. When the war boys returned with their booty, Canray Phemah, told him to be careful because the Komah people whose relatives the war boys had killed would try to revenge. William had not known about this, but said he would give the matter some consideration.

Not long after, Brimah and Moranu, sons of Mahmoddu Karimo of the Bompeh District came to see William and said that they wanted to join him so that they could avenge the wrongs in a decision which the chief had given in a case between Brimah and J.V. King of Tombo. Williams agreed at this time to have Brimah and others join him. He immediately dispatched Ndambah to Mende country for the remainder of his war boys. He also sent word to Canray Phemah informing him that he (William) was quite prepared now and that he (Canray) did not need to join him.

Thomas Koogbah jr, a younger brother of William's, came to and asked him why he was preparing for war. William told him not to worry. This war he was preparing for was in his own behalf. He was older than Thomas Neale, and of superior birth. He should have been the chief, but instead of ruling over his people, he allowed Thomas Neale Caulker, the son of a bondswoman to rule. When he heard this, Thomas Koogba jr understood the problem. He thanked William for the information and promised to render his services. He returned to Sankone and to Mannah Nhohbo at Mocobo, Cargbor, to ask for war boys so that he could assist his cousin. He succeeded in getting war boys from Peeh Boye, Sotelang and Nharmahwar. He then went to Sogbamene from whom he asked for any amount of money he could get, so that if the war did begin, he would have money with him and would not run into trouble. Sogbamene got salt in the amount of £3 and handed it to Bureh Kindo of Mopayleh to send to Thomas Koogba. But Bureh Kindo refused.

Thomas then went over to Peeh Lahkole of Thombay, and told him that he was about to defend his rights and it was necessary for Peeh to do all he could to help him, so could he kindly do everything possible to supply him with money and war boys. Peeh Lahkole would have agreed to this request had it not been for the interference of Sehy Gbasay who pointed out that they were outside the Shengeh District and if the owners of Shenge district, were bent on disturbing the peace of their country, it was their business to remain neutral. He further said that all he knew was that, if there were a dispute between people of the same district, all they had to do was to appeal to neighbouring chiefs for their assistance, which would probably be given. Although Thomas Koogbah persisted in his request for help, he failed. So he remained at Thombay for sometime. He even went to Mr. J.H. Pratt, the agent for S.B.A. Macfoy, William's old employer, and asked for assistance, telling him that if he could help them theret was a possibility that they could prevent the war from spreading to his factory. Not surpisingly Mr. Mcfoy refused to help.

Moses Lefevre who was in a small village near Thombay, was the only person who agreed to help him. He gave him goods to the value of 30 shillings. But Thomas' presence at Thombay made the inhabitants uneasy and they fled to other districts. When he realized that he was alone in the town, he returned to Sankone. Although he did not succeed in getting much money to help his cousin, he had been able to get many war boys from Bagroo, Cargbor and Imperreh. Since war boys depended on the booty they could get in a very short period from looting, the came in droves and Sankone soon became a very strong garrison.

During this time, Canray Phemah and others had been making preparations to assist William Caulker. Ndambah too had returned with the reserved war boys. But on their way to Mambo they had raided Gbanthee, a Temne Village. This caused the Temnes to be very angry, and they planned to take their revenge when Ndambah and his war boys returned, since Gbanthee was near the only road to the Mende country.

When William Caulker heard what Ndambah had done, he had him arrested and sent him over to the British Government, and Karimo took a cow to the Temnes in an attempt to appease them for Ndambah's actions. He told them that they depended on them to defend their rights. The Temnes accepted the peace offering and held their peace. From the 26th May to 16th June all was quiet, and most of the people who had sought refuge in different places returned home.

Regent Chief Thomas Neale Caulker had informed the Colonial Government of what William Caulker had done in Larwahmah and

Mambo and also reported the war preparation he was making. When no reply came from the Colonial Government he was somewhat confused. Meanwhile, the Reverend D.F. Wilberforce, a missionary of the United Brethren in Christ Church (UBC), a native of the Imperreh District, who was at Shengeh in charge of the Rufus Clark Training School, took measures to get some warriors from his native country for self defence, in case the war boys crossed over to Shengeh.

When a commandant at Bonthe, Sherbro heard of the war threat of war, he came over with constables and placed them in pairs in the principal towns on the border of the Tucker River.

Kong Gborgbor alias Kong Doomahbey, Chief of Mando sent Francis Caulker, Beah Lehbee and Gbannah Yormah as ambassadors to William Caulker to find out the reason for the war and to ask if he would be willing to meet with his cousin to discuss terms of peace. The ambassadors passed by Shengeh and asked the chief what the caused the problem. Chief Thomas Neale Caulker told them that he had not wronged his cousin in any way, but that as soon as he became regent chief, when he found out that his cousin was in trouble, he did all he could and was able to get him released. If he had in any way offended William, he (the chief), was willing to be reconciled. They went on to Mambo and found most of the war boys just crossing over to Shengeh District by way of connoloh. After making the necessary ceremony, William Caulker sent a slave with some money to give to the ambassadors. They were to give it to Kong Gborgbor to keep him quiet so that he would not interfere. William was determined to bring this long contention between himself and his cousin to a close and was not going to change his mind. The ambassadors returned by way of Shengeh, but did not tell the chief what his cousin had said. They continued their journey homeward and passed at Bompehtoke. Beah Lehbee, one of the ambassadors, secretly reported the state of affairs, as he saw it at Mambo, and the determination of William Caulker, to his cousin John Williams alias Commodore, and urged him to leave at once. Mr. Williams, was not willing to leave the country, without giving the information to the chief. And sent a messenger to inform him of the news he received from one of the ambassadors. After the chief received the information, he wrote a letter to William Caulker asking him his intentions—whether he was for peace or for war, so that he would know just what to do. Willie Caulker, son of George Caulker II, another of William's cousins, volunteered to take this letter. As soon as he reached Connoloh he met some war boys who had crossed over, and others were in the process of crossing. When they found that he was a Caulker of the Shengeh District he was captured and would have been killed, because his father was the cause of enmity between William Caulker and his cousin; but because he had been kind to William during his trouble at Shengeh in 1878, and William's mother had been sympathetic towards him, William had given instructions to the war boys that in case Willie Caulker or any of his children were caught, he was not to be killed, but was to be brought to him. So he was sent to William at Gbahongah, where he had moved his troops, and he was set him free. But he was afraid to return to Shengeh because of the treat of war.

The chief had still not heard from the Colonial Government; and because this state of affairs made him nervous and confused he made no move to go anywhere for refuge, but was determined to die where he was rather seek refuge anywhere.

News reached Shengeh on the 16th of June that the war boys had crossed and were plundering, taking captives and killing some in the upper districts. When Mr. Wilberforce, heard the same news, he went with some others to Shengeh town and did all they could to persuade Chief Thomas Neale Caulker to move to the mission for refuge, since all the people had deserted Shengeh and fled. But he absolutely refused. Seeing his determination, they forced him to at least go to East Bourne's Grove which was near by. Not more than five minutes after reaching East Bourne's Grove, they heard the war alarm and the plundering, killing and capturing. The war boys had much to plunder, but very few people to capture and only one person to kill, named Joseph Will. The war boys tried to take possession of the mission, and had as their general a head warrior by the name of Combay. Rev. D.F. Wilberforce had a head warrior by the name of Oatah Agbaray, and William Caulker had ordered his head warrior to bring along the head of Thomas Neale Caulker, the left hand and right breast of Mrs. Neale Caulker and the head of Rev. J. Gomer, and destroy the mission entirely. when they captured Shengeh. So when the war boys came to the mission, they fought desperately in order to keep that charge. There were about ten or twelve police constables with ammunition and a few other armed men as well.

When the warriors reached the mission, they had a white cloth tied to a pole which they hoisted up in place of a white flag. Through an interpreter who could speak the English language, they said they were for peace, and not for war. They were told to come near, if they were for peace; but they would not do it, instead one of them shot at the men on the verandah of the mission house. A few minutes later, another shot was heard, and this made it clear that they were for war. The men in the mission responded and the enemies began to retrace their steps. They were pursued until they reached near Gomer's Memorial Church, where they held their ground for a little. When reinforcements came from East Bourne's Grove, headed by Oatah Agbaray, they fled until they reached Mobetty's Beach, where they were joined by a reserve force of war boys with whom they waited.

While they were waiting, their head warrior, Combay began to approach the mission warriors. Oatah Agbaray then asked to be allowed to fight with Combay, so that they could see what he was capable of doing. He told them that they send a witness but that no one should fire at the other combatant. Two of the mission warriors, Miller Williams, an apprentice blacksmith of the mission, and H. Josephus Williams, then master of the mission day school at Shengeh, followed and stood about twenty-four feet from the spot where these two great warriors met in open combat. They struggled for about ten minutes when Oatah Agbaray cut off Combay's right hand, which made him to become furious, and he continued the combat for he was a Benjamite, as if he were not wounded. The hand that was cut off fell not very far from the two mission warriors and Miller, seeing it, lost courage and shot Combay in the temple, and he fell dead without a struggle. His war boys, seeing this fled and were pursued and shot at as far as Mparth. This was the first attack when one of their chief warriors was killed. The mission warriors, returned and cut off Combay's head. They took it to East Bourne's Grove, as a trophy of victory. This battle lasted about four hours. But the mission boys did not return till the next day which was Sunday. At the usual hour for Divine Services, the Rev. J. Gomer ordered the bell to be rung, but Mr. Wilberforce said he feared the war boys might take advantage of this and overtake them in church, and so advised that Divine Service be held in the mission headquarters and at East Bourne's Grove.

After the service, Joseph Will, who had been wounded the day before, died, and the mission warriors and refugees were burying him. During the burial ceremony, the war boys seized the opportunity to attack. This interrupted the funeral and prevented completion of the interment. Every one had to prepare for battle. The mission people were armed with swords, matchets, stick harpoons, flint-lock guns and cap guns. Both policemen and mission warriors were soon engaged in battle at Mo Tucker. As soon as the battle began, it began to drizzle, but every man kept his ground for a while, but it finally came down to a hand-to-hand fight, since the rain quickly became very heavy. Tommy, one of the mission men, was shot on the stomach, but fortunately the bullets did not penetrate. The man who shot him was instantly shot down by another of the mission men. His name was Lahsioo, a faithful servant of Mr. Franklin Caulker. Many others of William Caulker's men were shot and killed, making them to lose ground. The mission warriors and constables, had the advantage in the rain, because they were armed with snipes and breach loaders. The war boys had no choice but to retreat. They were chased and fired at to as far as Tresammah, Willie Caulker who, you remember was in their camp at Gbahwoongah, reported that the majority of them were killed, about none or ten of them died on the field. As the mission boys returned from chasing them, a few of the war boys were found hiding in the deserted houses at Shengeh. Farmah Gbondo, who was confronted by one of them, was in a hand to hand fight, which ended in a wrestle. If any other mission warrior had been near by, the war boy would have been killed or made a prisoner. This one however, fought very hard with Farmah Gbondo, but got out of his grip and mortally wounded him on the head. But for the best native treatment, Farmah Gbondo would have died.

The people in the mission became very watchful, and spies were posted in the dormer windows of the mission house to watch the movements of the war boys. Not long after the arrival of the mission warriors, those who were watching reported that they had seen the war boys passing by in pairs and hiding at Debia near the beach. The mission men at East Bourne thought it would be best to get all the water necessary for the mission house, in case they were surrounded, since the well was between East Bourne and Debia. It was then a matter of risk, since some of the war boys were also hiding near the well. Some people volunteered to guard those who would carry the water. Among the volunteers were the chief's brother, Mr. Allen E. Caulker, Saisay Boye of Shengeh, Gbannah Ville of Ncarthah and Rev. H.J. Williams, now Pastor of Otterbein Circuit, Bompehtoke. They went and returned, without encountering the enemy.

The number of war boys continued to swell as their reinforcements arrived, so some of the mission men from East Bourne, well armed with breach-loading rifles and shot guns, decided to stay near the well so that they could watch the movements of the enemy. When the war boys realized that there was no other way by they could pass and hide, all of them came on the beach about fifty yards across from the well and, as is customary in native wars, began to use abusive language, challenging the mission men to come over to them. This continued for about twenty minutes, during which time the mission men sent a column to the bush on the other side of the beach, to try and surround the enemy. Suddenly one of the mission men near the well fired at the enemy. The enemy returned the fire and meant to keep their ground, but noticed the column of mission men who had been sent to the beach approaching them and they were in danger of being surrounded. So they tried to flee but were chased. It was good to see them as they ran away, for the majority of them were carrying the booty they had obtained by plundering,—boxes, bundles of country clothes, bundles of English goods, etc. As the mission men drew near, about N'carthy, they began to throw away the goods which they were tryng to take into the bush for safety. The mission men took possession of the things and returned. When they reached East Bournes's Grove with the things they had recovered from the war boys, they found out that some of the goods belonged to Mrs. Lucia Caulker of Debia. The things were returned to her, and those things which had not been claimed were kept as trophies. This was the end of William Caulker's war at Shengeh. Perhaps they would have regrouped for another attempt to attack the mission, but a man-of-war was sighted off the Plantain Island and a few of the marines came ashore and found that the enemy had fled. And so William Caulker failed to get the head of Rev. J. Gomer, the left hand and right breast of Mrs. Neal and head of Chief Thomas Neale Caulker.

But the reader must not forget that although William Caulker's war boys did not succeed in carrying out his wishes at Shengeh and the mission, those who went to the other districts in Plantain and Shengeh territory did great injury to life and property, beginning from Bendoo right on to Bompeh Candor in the interior. Thombah District lost seventy-nine people who were captured and killed. All of the thirty-five towns which made up the district were burned. Among the influential ones killed were Beah Gbortoy, who was a sub-chief, and Mengee Howeh Gbain, son of the old sub-chief Bah Kirkle. At Manoh, a good many people were captured, the number of which we are not able to give, but thirty-seven of these were rescued by the English Government and sent home. One of those rescued was a young lady, a Mrs. Taylor, who had only been married for about three months before the war broke out. She and her husband, had come from Kissy to spend their honeymoon with a relative, Mrs. Frank Dixon, wife of Mr. Frank Dixon, a school teacher. A Mammy Davies and her husband Bamp and a girl named Konah and others. An influential man named Saisay Minto, who had resisted when he was caught, was butchered to death. In Bompehtoke District, those who were killed were Gborkeyor of Bowmah,. A little over forty people were captured, but a few of them were released before the town was burned. The town of Bompehtoke was not burnt, due to the influence of Mormo Margbo, son of late Vandee Margbo of Tangarnemah, Bompeh District. The late Vandee, was a relative of the sub-chief, Kong Marthee. But a woman named Conyah Boye and her two children and an old woman were taken captive, and the town was plundered. Mr. J. N. Lefevre had just died, but his factory was still under the management of his son Moses Lefevre, The factory contained cotton goods, hardware, spirits, tobacco, rice, with many cows. The war boys took possession of these and the factory became their garrison. They subsisted on the rice, caattle and palm oil, etc., and for three days they remained on the spot till they were forced to leave when they spotted the man-of-war.

Before they reached Kooloong which is a mission station, they met Mr. J. Arthur Richards the pastor who had just returned from Bonthe. He was attempting to escape by boat, but, as the tide was out he could not leave. When the war boys saw his property in the boat, they relieved him of his goods and left him free without harming him. When the tide came in, he left the station in charge of a Mr. A. F. Campbell, who pretended to be a Sierra Leonean (from the colony). He was on very good terms with the war boys. Whenever they went out plundering, they returned with their loot and would give him some of it. He would in turn give them gifts of tobacco, etc. Some of the refugees who were in the bush would come out stealthily to him when it was dark, and find shelter overnight. Early the next morning they would return to their hiding places. Their properties were brought to him and placed under his care and he would pretend that they were his.

William Caulker, who was then at Gbahongah, had written letters to some of his friends in England and his wife Member, who was taking them to Bonthe disguised as a refugee, happened to get to Kooloong. She was well received by A.F. Campbell and a warm friendship was formed which resulted in her disclosing to him that she was bearing some letters to be posted at Bonthe for England. When Campbell saw from the addresses of these letters that they were addressed to some of the Lords in England, he secretly managed to read them and found that the contents were something against the Colony of Sierra Leone. Knowing this, he removed the letters from the envelopes and filled them with papers. Next day the woman left for Bonthe.

Though Mr. A. F. Campbell pretended to be a Sierra Leonean, there were some marks on him which eventually betrayed him. After Member left, a war boy came to see Mr. Campbell and found that his property had increased. He realized that Campbell had more boxes than before. When asked about the extra boxes Mr. Campbell said, that he had brought them down from upstairs as he wanted to use them. When he turned his back, the war boys saw some marks on the back of his neck a little above the collar which they recognized as porroh markings. They immediately told him that they the marks did not belong to a Sierra Leonean but to a native, and that since he had been deceitful, he was to go outside and prepare for death. He pleaded that his mother was a native Temne and his father a Sierra Leonean. His plea made no difference. In a few minutes, everything in the mission house had been taken away. He was stripped of his clothing and ordered to get out of doors to be killed. He had no choice, but to take his bible which he held, and slowly marched down the steps to the spot where he was to be killed. Before starting out he asked the war boys to grant him the time and liberty to pray, and they allowed him to do so. After he arose from prayer he took his Bible and went down for his journey to the execution spot. As they marched to the spot, they sang their war song which meant death to any who was to be killed. Since Mr. Campbell, was a native, he knew this and kept close to his God. He reached the spot appointed for his execution, and the song ended. As the death blow was about to be struck, a man interrupted and asked that the matter be referred to Mormor, son of Vandee Margbah, who was their general, since the man claimed to be a Sierra Leonean, and orders had been given to them not to destroy the life of any Sierra Leonean. The matter was referred, and, Mormor knew Mr. Campbell through his brother Allie who was then a mission boy under Campbell's tutorage. He hastily gave orders that the prisoner should not be killed. So Campbell's life was spared and the war boys went away with all that they plundered from the mission house.

Those war boys who were still in Shengeh District where on their way to Bompehtoke. A column had taken the route to Messam, and when they reached Gehahoo they found only a few men found there. These men, knowing that the women who were escaping had not yet crossed over to the Thaimdale District, began to run towards Messam to report that the war boys were coming. Seeing that, the war boys, followed and gave full chase to one of them named Ngar-nhe, who ran with such a speed that he fell down and remained in that position for about eighteen hours. The war boys found the body, felt it, and decided that he was dead. So they continued their pursuit of the others. That delay gave the men from Gehahoo the opportunity to reach Messam, and give the alarm that the war boys were coming. Since the canoes were ready, the people hastily boarded them. But, the canoes could not contain them all. So some had to stay in the water alongside of the canoes and be held up by some of those in the canoes. Some of those in the water held on to the sides of the canoes. That is how they crossed over to the other side of the river, which is a distance of about half a mile. When the war boys reached the town some tried to chase the last canoes by swimming, and they would have overtaken them, but fortunately they had no guns, while those who were in the canoes had guns which they made use of. The pursuing war boys were forced to return.

A little girl of fourteen years old named Kafway Nassy who was still in the town and was pursued by the war boys, but since she was a fast runner, they failed to catch her. She did not run very far before she hid herself in the bush. The war boys searched and searched for her, but they could not find her, so they returned to the town leaving her hidden from Saturday till Tuesday afternoon, when she saw Moses Lefevre who was coming from Thombay to look for some of his people. Kafway was then finally able to come out of her hiding place.

From Saturday to Tuesday the war boys remained at Messam using their skill to make captives of those who landed there as refugees trying to cross over to the Thaimdale District.

I too would have been caught. On that same Saturday, I was returning from a business trip to Bonthe. As we approached Mando Banks, we noticed many people about ten of them, in small canoes. All of Shengeh land was in smoke, and not knowing what it meant, I thought we had better land at Messam to ascertain what was really happening. As I had taken refuge at Thombay, my boys with cattle and other property were still at Bompehtoke. As I came close to the shore, I noticed that all the war boys were hiding. Someone in a small canoe was saying to me, "George, don't land there; the war boys are there." When I turned to see who had said that, I found that it was Mr. John Williams. So we turned for the Tucker River and I got to Thombay. There I met my boys who had escaped from Bompehtoke, but had left my property behind.

On the following Sunday morning, news reached us at Thombay that the war boys had crossed over to Gbampeneh on the other side of the Tucker River, and had seized the property of most of the Shengeh people who had sought refuge there. Mrs. Phillipa Dillet, daughter of Paramount Chief Thomas Neale Caulker was among the captives on this occasion, other captives were Kene Mammah of Salt Pond and Humpah Ndayloy of Bowmah.

This is how Kene Mammah and Humpah Ndayloy were captured at Sessam. After escaping with some of their people at Gbampeneh, they returned by boat, to look for the rest of their people. The war boys came upon them and captured them. They were then told that, if they did not take them over and show them where their people were hidden, they would be killed. The two men were obliged to take them over and show them where the refugees had hidden in Gbampeneh. The news of the war boys taking possession of Gbampeheh caused panic at Thombay, and the people fled to neighboring places. Some went to Gbehan, some to Bagru, and some to Imperreh, others crossed over Bonthe which is situated on the opposite side near the mouth of the Tucker River which makes it difficult for people to get from Thombay to the sea.

Joseph Domingo, who had a factory at Lacole was about to go down the river, to get one of the mission boats "Olive Branch" or "May Gomer" to come to Thombay and take his goods to Bonthe. He arranged to go down in a small canoe with a young man, who lived with him, named Kosoko. This young man, dreaded an encounter with the enemy down the river, was reluctant to go. J. Domingo, in an attempt to outwit him, asked him take his box down to the canoe. The young man was suspicious of the plan and was unwilling to do as he was bidden. By now, all the women and children had left for various places, leaving behind the men who had killed all the cattle and poultry and were cooking, so that they could eat them before seeking refuge. They did not want to leave all the cattle and chickens at the mercy of the war boys. This feast was partly what made Kosoko reluctant to go, as he had no intention of leaving the feast behind. J. Domingo, realizing that the young man was reluctant to leave, seized him and tried to take him down by force, but the young man screamed at the top of his lungs. This alarmed the men who were preparing for their feast and assumed that it was the war boys. Everyone deserted the town to save his life. J. Domingo, who was the cause of the panic, quietly left the scene which he had created. He went down to the river alone, and when he realized that all the men had left, he returned to pick up his things and left for Bonthe.

Thombay town itself had been fortified by an employee of S.B.A. Macfoy, named Pratt, alias Mendi Mahoo, who had a warrior named Gbanjavura. That night, some refugees from the Shengeh District had swum over to Thombay, to notify the town that the war boys were collected in a town called Sankone, under Thomas Koogbah Caulker, and were preparing to come to Thombay to raid Mr. Pratt's factory. When they heard the news all the men gathered in one spot. That night, people were heard calling from the opposite side of Thombay, begging to be taken across the river. The people of Thombay ignored then. But they continued to beg, saying that they were refugees from Shengeh country who had been captured by the war boys. They had been able to escape but were afraid of being captured again. The Thombay people still refused to believe their story. Thinking they were just a party of the war boys, they waited till the morning at which time a strong escort was dispatched to cross them over.

Due to the unrest which was caused by the invasion of Gbampeneh, caused Chief Kong Gbogbor to go over to Thombay where he met the people who had just been brought over. He cross examined them, but was not satisfied with their answer. So he sent them over to Bonthe in Custody of the chief's son, Jabez Doomahbey, and G. M. Domingo. Bonthe. Their names were Bowome, Sogbamem of Kompoh, Bureh Kindo of Paileh, Jehehbye of Paileh. They were arrested because on interrogation, it was discovered that they had already been interviewed by Thomas Koogbah Caulker, who got them to give him a certain amount of money in exchange for their freedom. Upon examination at Bonthe there was not sufficient evidence to incriminate them, so they were released.

When I returned to Thombay from Bonthe, I was given the news that the war boys at Sankone had dispersed when they heard that a man of war had arrived at Shengeh. They were so desperate to escape that they killed the strong captives whom they had, because they afraid that they would not be able to force them to go with them. One of the unfortunate victims was a very kind-hearted man by name Beah Gbortoi of Thombah. Seye Killy and Thuah Barlay would have been killed also, but Thomas Koogbah Caulker stopped them. They carried away most of the people of the town, including Sierra Leoneans (those from the Colony) and property including some which was owned by Thomas Caulker, and his cousin Charles's children who were in the town. This made Thomas follow them as far as to Yahpomah where Commandant Garrett had stationed policemen. At Yahpmah, he learnt that he couldnot get any help, as the policemen there had been instructed not to interfere with that the Bompeh branch of the war.

On the next afternoon after my arrival, a steam launch arrived at Thombay. Captain Halkett came ashore with Mr. H.J. Williams and

Thomas Kainey, as pilots, with fifty constables. Captain Halket asked me r lodging and I was happy to give him room and board in our villa.

After taking a bath and eating, Captain Halkett called me, wanting to get information about the war. I gave him the names of the ringleaders and the necessary particulars. Thomas Caulker, I said, could be found about Yahpomah. William Caulker, Kene Fumoh, Muranah, Crimebah Alias Karimu, were somewhere in the Bompeh District. He asked me how I gotten my information and I told him that I was at Thombay when Thomas Caulker went and called a meeting with Chief Bah Lacole, Seye Gbasay and others of his principal men. He told them that he gad gone to meet with and try to dissuade his brother William from waging war, but William had told him to get away, because this time he was going to fight for his own benefit. After all, as the elder cousin, he should be reigning instead of his younger cousin Thomas Neale Caulker, whose head he said he was going to bring back as a trophy. Understanding the reason for the war, Thomas Koogbah jr had decided he would help his brother. So he called these men together and asked for help of either money or men, adding that this would also render their district safe from the disturbance by the war boys. He told them to choose the lesser of two evils. I also told Captain Halkett that the war boys had also captured several Sierra Leoneans, all of whom might be recovered, if he went, as I suggested, towards Yahpomah. The Captain asked me to accompany him, but since Gbanjavura, had killed my goats, I was on my way to Bonthe to issue a summons against him.

When I returned from Bonthe, I learned that Captain Halkett had captured Thomas Caulker in the Gargbor District and recovered some of the captives, all of whom were sent to town.

A woman named Charlotte Hingston was the reason for William Caulker's capture. This woman had been living with him as a wife and had stayed with him during the war. She got rich from the booty of palm oil, kola nuts, etc. which the war boys brought in. When the war ended, she talked William Caulker into getting her a boat which would take her to Freetown with her produce. When she got to Freetown, she went to the police immediately and gave information about William to the police. They immediately told Mr. Lawson where Mr. Caulker could be found. William Caulker was captured in a small village called Gbawonga, in the Shengeh territory. After his arrest, Karimu, Murana, Beah High, Richard Canray Bah Caulker and Lahigh, were arrested in the Bompehtoke territory. Sir Samuel Lewis, William's old friend and former attorney was the prosecutor of the case. About this time I received a communication from Captain North Daniel, who was in charge of the detachment at Shengeh stating that I was to appear in Freetown in connection with the case, on behalf of the prosecution. I went to Shengeh to meet Captain Halkett, whom I asked for a way to get to Freetown. But he told me to get a boat. Since this was not possible, I returned to Thombay. Not long after that, I received word from the captain him that a launch was ready to take me to Freetown. I returned to Shengeh where I boarded the launch for Freetown.

END OF THE CAULKER MANUSCRIPTS

Resources

Books

Fitzjohn, William Rev.—**"Ambassador of Christ and Caesar"**—Dayton Press, Ibadan 1975

Fyfe Christopher—**"A History of Sierra Leone"**—Oxford University Press, 1962

Fyfe Christopher—**"A History of Sierra Leone"**—Gregg Revivals, Hampshire England, 1993.

Fyfe, Christopher—**"Sierra Leone Inheritance"**—London University Press 1964

Goddard, T.N. **"The Handbook of Sierra Leone**—Negro Universal Press, N.Y.,1925, Reprint 1925

Hall, H.U.—**"The Sherbro of Sierra Leone"**—A preliminary Report on the work of the University Museum's Expedition to West Africa, 1937. Philadelphia: The University press, University of Pennsylvania, 1938

Kup, A.P.—**"Sierra Leone, A Concise History"** New York—St Martin's Press, 1975

Kup. A.P.—**"Sierra Leone 1400-1787"**—Cambridge at the University Press, 1961

Mills J.S. Rev. **"Africa"** Dayton Ohio, United Brethren Publishing House, 1898

Louise, E.—"**Elizabeth Hardcastle 1741-1808—A Lady of color in South Carolina Low Country**" Phoenix Publishers, Columbia, South Carolina 2001.

St. Clair, William—"**The Door of No Return—The History of Cape Coast Castle and the Atlantic Slave Trade**" Blue Ridge, New York, 1999

Tower, Lionel—**"A Short Story of Kagbor"** not published

Turnbul, Colin—**"The Lonely African"**—Long Island City, N.Y. 1962

Articles

Domingo, George Maximillian **"Caulker Manuscripts"**—Sierra Leone Studies Part 1—October 1920, pp29-48. Part II-July 1925, pp1-8

Carter, Don and Vreugdenhul—**"Protestant Missionary Endeavours in Sierra Leone**" Installment 5, 1/5/200

Caulker Francis,—Excerpt from his book "The Caulkers—**Slavery, the African Experience, And the African-American Experience**" unpublished

Caulker, Richard,—**"Christian Experience in an African Christian Family"** The World Evangel, Youth Issue, May 1952

Caulker Stephen BarThebin—**"Brief history of the Caulkers"**—Caulker Descendants' Reunion Booklet 1999.

Karefa-Smart John Dr.—" **Vignettes From the Memoirs of a Bompeh Caulker"**—Caulker Descendants' Reunion Booklet 2001

Mauser, Bruce L.—**"African Academy—Clapham 1799-1806 "**—history of Education, January 2004, No 1: 87-103

National Archives—Black Presence—**"Africa and the Atlantic Slave Trade"**—10/9/06 www.nationalarchives.gov.uk/pathways/blackhistory.africa_caribbean/afric_trade.h . . . 10/9/2006

Opala, Joseph—**"Bunce island, Historical Summary"**—9/20/2004

Resource Bank of Africans in America—"Royal African Company Established"—The terrible Transformation, Part 1 1450-2750. www.pbs.org/wgbh/aia/part1p269.html

Shuey, W.J.—"Journal of Sierra Leone Travels—1855

Otterbein College Publication—**African Prince Educated at Otterbein**

James T Scott—editor, Feature

Reeck, Darrell—**"Mary and Joseph Gomer—Extending the Spirit of Armistad in Sierra Leone"**—Historical Bulleting of the world Methodist Historical Society, Vol 27, Third Quarter 1998

Sierra Leone Archives, Fourah Bay College

Picture Gallery

Some of the Pillars in our Family

James Canreba, Son of Thomas Kon Tham
Chief of Bompeh 1842-1857
Christopher Fyfe—Inheritance (1964)

Paramount Chief Alphonso Theophilus Caulker of Kagboro
Chiefdom 1933-1954
Son of George Stephen II, Brother of Lulu Caulker of Mambo
Father of Gladys Lefevre, Ellen Caulker, John Caulker, Doris
Lenga-Kroma, Olivia Caulker, Mildred Caulker, Tennyson Caulker

Children of PC AT.Caulker

Gladys Lefevre, Mother of Annie, Dwight, Lucy John Caulker, Father of Lucianne, Ellen Caulker (see below)

Olivia Caulker, Mother of Swinton, Yema, Brian, Luba

Valecious and Ellen Caulker
Parents of Thomas, Valena, A.T., Abraham (Bobby)

George Augustus Caulker, son of Francis Caulker of Mambo

Lulu Caulker—Daughter of Franklyn Caulker of Shenge,
Wife of George Augustus Caulker of Mambo
Sister of PC A.T.Caulker and Kai Caulker
Mother of Rachel, Albert, Richard, Solomon, Bunting, Glen,
Amelia Francis, Stephen.

Children of George and Lulu Caulker

Rachel & Amelia

Front—Richard & Albert
Back—Bunting & Solomon

Rachel
Mother of Lulu & Genevieve
Richard

Father of Imodale, Lucilda, Smita(Elaine),
Velma, Richard, Sheila

Albert

Solomon
Father of Ferne & Karron

Glen, Father of Glenna, Glen &Gerard

Bunting, Father of Regina

Amelia

Rachel

Richard

Glen

Amelia

Susan Kai-Sha Caulker—Daughter of Franklyn Caulker, sister of Lulu and Michael M.Caulker. Mother of Rhoda, Flora, Dulcie, Marie, Adeline

Children of Susan Kai-Sha Caulker

Paramount Chief Marie Bunting Zizer of Mattru Jong—daughter of Susan Kaisha Caulker.

Rhoda Massalay
Mother of Martha & Victoria

Flora Myers
Mother of Sunbeam, Elsie Mae,
Lawrence Stephen Laurel, Albert Chico

**Dulcie Bundu
Williams**

Adeline

Paramount Chief Madam Honoria Bailor—
Caulker of Kagboro Chiefdom—1961-1999
Mother of Marvin. Hilton, Esther, Chadwick and Chico

Max Bailor son of Mary Caulker-Bailor

Eva Caulker—Mama Hota
Daughter of Benson Caulker
Mother of Doyle Sumner, Marion, Millicent, Irene

Children of Eva Caulker

Marion Jalloh-Jamboria

Doyle Sumner

Mabel Caulker—Daughter of Chief Thomas Canreba-Caulker of Bompeh Chiefdom
Mother of Thomas Obai, John, Betty, Yebu, Maude and Frank

Children of May Caulker Karefa-Smart

Betty Karefa Smart
Mother of Akim, Maude Marie, Maude, Foyoh, Theresa May, Alfred, (Kenke)

Thomas Obai Karefa-Smart
Father of Peter, Thomas, Charles

John Karefa-Smart
Father of Rosa Lee, John, Suzanne

Maude Karefa-Smart	Yebu Karefa-Smart

Other Caulker Ancestors

Rev. D.H. Caulker Son of Chief Thomas Stephen Caulker of Kagboro
Pastor in Kono until his death at age 113
Grandfather of Rev. David H. Caulker

Grace Caulker
Daughter of Rev Michael M.Caulker
Mother of Esther, Sylvia, Cyril

Martha Sumner-Ford
Daughter os Susan Rose
Neale-Caulker
Mother of Maisie, Enid,
Michael, Winston

Tuzylline Williams of Bonthe mother of Dr.Arthur Williams

Gabriel Deen—Son of Sally Caulker
Grandson of Francis Caulker of Mambo
Father of Salimatu and Marie

Melvina Caulker-Challobah-Bonthe
Mother of Melvyn Challobah and his siblings

Rev. Dr. William Henry Fitzjohn
Grandson of Katherine Caulker
Father of Amelia, Dwight, William, Kwame, Walter, Katie, Jonathan

Charles Caulker—son of George Stephen CaulkerII of Plantain / Shenge chiefdom
Rachel Caulker, Daughter of PC A.G.Caulker of Bumpeh chiefdom
Parents of Princess, Annie, Phlorence, Melvyn

Andrew Owen Caulker,
Grandson of Thomas Stephen Caulker of Kagboro
Father of Patrick, Jasper, Dwight, Enid, Lawrence

Nora Yanni,
Daughter of Chief A.G. Caulker of Bumpeh
Mother of Edward, John, Maria, Arthur

GIVING SERVICE TO THEIR COUNTRY
FORMER FIRST LADY

Patricia Tucker-Kabba
Granddaughter of Charles Caulker son of Francis Caulker of Mambo

THE AMBASSADORS

Dr. William H. Fitzjohn and Preident John F. Kennedy

Dr. Richard E. Kelfa-Caulker and President John F. Kennedy

THE STATESMAN

Sir, Milton Margai, Prime Minister with Dr. John Karefa-Smart

In the rising of the sun and its going down,
We remember our Ancestors,
So long as we live, they too shall live.
As we remember them

Author's Bio

Imodale Caulker-Burnett, seen here with the Staff of Office of the newlyly crowned Chief of Kagboro Chiefdom, Rev. Doris Lega Caulker Gbabior II (2010), was born in Freetown, Sierra Leone, West Africa. She was the first child of Richard and Olivette Kelfa-Caulker, and the third grandchild of George and Lulu Caulker of Mambo, Kagboro Chiefdom.

She is a retired Certified Family Nurse Practitioner, Healing Touch Practitioner, and Substance Abuse Consultant. She has also been a piano teacher and assistant organist.

She was educated at Teachers College, Columbia University, in New York,—Masters Degree in Nursing Education (1985).

New York Hospital, Cornell University,—Certificate as a Family Nurse Practitioner (1973).

Presbytarian Hospital School of Nursing, Columbia University, New York—BS Nursing (1965)

Otterbein College Westerville, Ohio—BS Zoology (1963)

Annie Walsh Memorial School, Freetown, Sierra Leone. 1957)

She worked as a staff nurse in the Presbytarian Hospital, Visiting Nurse Service of New York, Family Care Group Practice, in St Luke's hospital, and Substance Abuse Consultant, at the Medical College of Virginia.

In 1999, with the help of two cousins, she founded the Caulker Descendants Association, US. Annual reunions are now held where members meet new aunts, uncles, and cousins, learn about family history, try to learn the tribal language (Sherbro) and just have fun as a family.

Since her retirement in 2003, she has gone home to Sierra Leone annually to oversee the work of her Community Development Organization—Lesana, which is working on development and rehabilitation of her father's birth place, Mambo Town, Mambo Section, Kagboro Chiefdom, Moyamba District.

She lives in Richmond Virginia, with her husband Clive Burnett.

Edwards Brothers,Inc!
Thorofare, NJ 08086
01 December, 2010
BA2010335